To Mary —

COOKING WITH JACK
The New Jack Daniel's Cookbook

LYNNE TOLLEY & MINDY MERRELL

Cheers!
Tolley
Lynne

d Hill Street Press
Athens, Georgia

A HILL STREET PRESS BOOK

Published in the United States of America by Hill Street Press LLC
191 East Broad Street, Suite 216 • Athens, Georgia 30601-2848 USA • 706-613-7200
info@hillstreetpress.com • www.hillstreetpress.com

Hill Street Press is committed to preserving the written word. Every effort is made to print books on acid-free paper with post-consumer recycled content.

The recipes in this book require careful preparation and the use of proper ingredients. Neither the author nor publisher assumes any liability for the preparation and/or consumption of food prepared using the recipes in this book.

Hill Street Press books are available in bulk purchase and customized editions to institutions/companies.

Text design: Brandi Goodson • Cover design: Jeff Porter • Back cover photography: David Bailey
Photographs on pages 59, 99, courtesy of Lynne Tolley. Photograph on page 61 © Archie Liberman.
Photographs on pages 2, 44 © 2006 Jack Daniel's Properties, Inc. All other photographs by Eric England © 2006 Jack Daniel's Properties, Inc. All rights reserved.

Library of Congress Cataloging-in-Publication Data
Tolley, Lynne, 1950-
 Cooking with Jack : the new Jack Daniels cookbook / Lynne Tolley & Mindy Merrell.
    p. cm.
 Includes index.
 ISBN-13: 978-1-58818-119-0 (alk. paper)
 ISBN-10: 1-58818-119-7 (alk. paper)
 1. Cookery (Whiskey) 2. Cocktails. I. Merrell, Mindy. II. Title.
 TX726.T64 2006
 641.2'52--dc22

                          2006026931

ISBN-10: 1-58818-119-7
ISBN-13: 978-1-58818-119-0

10 9 8 7 6 5 4 3 2 1

First printing

FOR MOTHER
The best country cook I know

Acknowledgements

WE OFFER OUR THANKS

To Margaret Tolley and Leola Dismukes
who taught Lynne how to cook;

To Debbie Baxter, Lynne's right hand,
who keeps Miss Mary's running so smoothly;

To Tom Brown who keeps Lynne happy;

To R.B. Quinn who kept things organized
and us laughing;

To Judy Long and Tom Payton of Hill Street Press
who made this project a pleasure;

To John Hayes of Jack Daniel's who encouraged and
supported this book;

To Eric England who made such
beautiful photographs;

To the cooks, hostesses and servers who
for generations have fed so many at Miss Mary
Bobo's Boarding House; and

To all our guests.

Contents

Introduction

My mother, Margaret Tolley, is the best country cook I know. She grew up in Fayetteville, Tennessee, just down the road from our home in Lynchburg where we live today. My daddy, the late Jim Tolley, always said he'd hit the jackpot with Mother. He loved her cooking as much as he loved her.

My older brother, Jimmy Lee, and I feel the same way about Mother. We grew up in her kitchen, talking, laughing, helping, getting underfoot. She's always been a happy, joyful woman and it comes through in everything she cooks.

Thanks to her our lives have been filled with fresh homegrown vegetables, locally cured country ham, fresh sausage, and chicks pecking in the backyard. We picked turnip greens in the back field, poke sallet along the fencerow and blackberries wherever they grew. For years Mother canned her late summer tomatoes and the most delicious tomato juice. To this day, she puts up fresh corn in the freezer to keep us in fried corn all year long. Her homemade desserts, like towering fresh coconut cakes, strawberry shortcake with flaky pastry, and the most elaborate congealed salads, are beyond compare. Our friends all over Moore County anxiously await her Christmas divinity with black walnuts. No one can top her fried chicken.

Our tiny town of Lynchburg is a rural agricultural community with a population of less than 500 tucked in the hollows of Middle Tennessee. It's home to generations of good country cooks and even better eaters. But, that's probably not why you recognize the name. Most folks know of Lynchburg because the name is printed on every single bottle of Jack Daniel's Tennessee Whiskey. My Great-Grand Uncle Jack's whiskey is one of the bestselling whiskies the world over. Every drop is crafted here in Lynchburg, just as it was in his day.

Whiskey making has been going on around here even before Uncle Jack's time. Our hills were once dotted with distilleries on account of our pure spring water and the abundance of corn and sugar maple. Daddy's family once owned the nearby Eaton and Tolley Distillery and both my Great Uncle Jess Motlow and my Uncle Lem Tolley were master distillers at Jack Daniel's, two of only six in the company's history. You could say whiskey making truly runs in my blood.

Since 1984, I've spent much of my time as the proprietress of Miss Mary Bobo's Boarding House just off Lynchburg's town square. Every day but Sunday we serve a midday dinner of two meats and six vegetables, homemade biscuits, rolls or cornbread, iced tea, coffee, and dessert in the old boarding house tradition. Our food is simple Tennessee country cooking. Guests dine family style at long tables spread throughout the old 1820s white clapboard house.

When I was a child, the Bobo Hotel was filled with folks who needed a place to call home. Miss Mary served her boarders and special guests three home-cooked meals a day. My family ate there when we were kids, but the boarding house wasn't a public restaurant as it is today. I often played around the boarding house as a child while Mother and Mary's daughter, Louise, ran the flower shop down the street. I recall the many times when Miss Mary stopped by the shop for an afternoon break and gossip session while Mother arranged flowers. After Miss Mary passed in 1983, just shy of the age of 102, I had the wonderful opportunity to succeed her as proprietress. We opened Miss Mary's as a boarding house-style restaurant and have been going strong ever since.

Visit on a Monday and we're likely to serve slow-cooked pot roast and skillet fried chicken and gravy, creamy mashed potatoes, speckled butter beans with sweet red pepper relish, a vegetable casserole or two, and homemade biscuits and gravy. We serve fried okra and Lynchburg candied apples every single day because our guests can't seem to get enough of them. For dessert there's fudge pie served with Jack Daniel's whipping cream. And that's just the Monday menu.

Each year Lynchburg welcomes more than 250,000 visitors from around the world. Most everyone tours the Distillery and many join us for dinner. I get such a kick out of introducing folks from Germany, Japan, and even Wisconsin, to grits, okra, and black-eyed peas. Many of their stories appear throughout these pages.

This book is the result of a life of good eating, cooking, entertaining, and sharing food with others. Legend has it that my Uncle Jack loved to host extravagant parties and feasts. He so enjoyed dancing with the ladies that he kept a ballroom in his home. Like Uncle Jack, we Lynchburg folks take our fun and our food seriously. Whether it's a twenty-four-hour pig roast, church supper, tailgate party, or dinner at home with a few neighbors, someone in Lynchburg is preparing a welcoming spread. Of course, Uncle Jack is still the life of the party.

Over the years my longtime friend, collaborator, and coauthor Mindy Merrell and I have cooked up friendships with talented home cooks, fancy chefs, and bartenders across the nation. These creative exchanges have enriched our own interpretations and love of Southern country cooking. We're pleased to share these recipes and the stories that inspired them, all of which draw together the time-tested traditions of Mother, Miss Mary, and my Uncle Jack. We all agree—a little Jack makes a whole lot of things taste better.

Lynne Tolley, Proprietress
Miss Mary Bobo's Boarding House
Lynchburg, Tennessee

JACK HOUR COCKTAILS

WE'RE
Tennessee Whiskey

Contrary to what many folks think, Jack Daniel's is not bourbon. Our whiskey enjoys an entirely different product classification called Tennessee Whiskey. It's made only in the hills of Middle Tennessee from a blend of corn, rye, barley malt, and iron-free water from the limestone Cave Spring. We do share a connection with bourbon, but we take the crucial extra step called charcoal mellowing. Before barrel aging, our whiskey travels through ten feet of hard sugar maple charcoal to give Jack Daniel's its characteristic smoothness. The whiskey is aged on the Moore County hillsides surrounding Lynchburg in newly charred white oak barrels.

JACK DANIEL'S OLD NO. 7 BLACK LABEL TENNESSEE WHISKEY

Our world-famous whiskey has been awarded seven international gold medals, including one for "world's best whiskey" given to Uncle Jack at the 1904 World's Fair in St. Louis, Missouri. His famous square bottle and handsome black and white label is recognized around the world because of what's inside—charcoal-mellowed Tennessee Whiskey, a well-balanced mix of caramel, vanilla, wood notes and a slightly fruity and distinctively dry finish.

GENTLEMAN JACK RARE TENNESSEE WHISKEY

My Uncle Jack experimented with double charcoal mellowing but never did much with it. In 1988, we decided to dig up his notes and give it a try. The result is Gentleman Jack Rare Tennessee Whiskey. It's made from a slightly different recipe and is the only whiskey in the world that is charcoal mellowed twice, once before and once again after the aging process. It has a silky finish laced with caramel, fruit, vanilla, and smoke. I like to call it our Tennessee cognac and often serve it in snifters after supper. And don't miss my favorite Classic Jack Mint Julep featuring Gentleman Jack (see page 13).

JACK DANIEL'S SINGLE BARREL TENNESSEE WHISKEY

Each barrel of Jack Daniel's has its own personality, a distinct nose, color, and taste. Single Barrel means just that. For this whiskey, Master Distiller Jimmy Bedford and a team of expert tasters pick exceptional barrels to be

bottled alone, without blending with whiskey from other barrels. These special barrels age on the upper floors of the barrel houses where the hot, humid Tennessee summers and cold winters create more movement of the whiskey in and out of the wood. The result is a rich amber, mature whiskey with heightened flavors of toasted oak, vanilla, and caramel. I love to give Single Barrel as a gift. Maybe that's why I get so many party invitations!

The beautiful view from BBQ Hill. That building on the left is one of the many Jack Daniel's barrel houses that dot the landscape around Lynchburg.

BUY YOUR OWN BARREL

Whiskey connoisseurs can place an order for an entire barrel of Jack Daniel's Single Barrel Tennessee Whiskey. Each barrel yields about 240 (750 ml) bottles. With the purchase, barrel owners get the bottled whiskey and the barrel that it was aged in, a customized metal neckband for each bottle, a brass plaque, and a framed certificate of ownership.

BEYOND THE CLASSICS,
my definition of a Manhattan expands to include all Jack Daniel's concoctions chilled and served straight up (no ice) in a cocktail glass. (Of course, many folks enjoy a Manhattan over ice in a rocks glass.) Lots of flavors combine well with Tennessee Whiskey, but the goal of these elegant offerings is never to mask it.

A well-stocked bar and a few simple tools are all you need for making great cocktails quickly. See "Setting up the Bar" on page 23.

Note that all cocktail recipes are for one serving unless otherwise indicated or for a punch recipe.

CLASSIC JACK MANHATTAN

★★★★★★★★★★★★★★★★★★★★★★★

2 ounces Jack Daniel's Tennessee Whiskey
1/2 ounce sweet vermouth
Dash of bitters

Combine all ingredients in a mixing glass with ice. Stir to chill. Strain into a chilled cocktail glass. Garnish with a maraschino cherry.

PERFECT GENTLEMAN JACK MANHATTAN

★★★★★★★★★★★★★★★★★★★★★★★

2 ounces Gentleman Jack Rare Tennessee Whiskey
1/4 ounce dry vermouth
1/4 ounce sweet vermouth
Dash of bitters

Combine all ingredients in a mixing glass with ice. Stir to chill. Strain into a chilled cocktail glass. Garnish with a lemon twist.

LICORICE MANHATTAN

★★★★★★★★★★★★★★★★★★★★★★★

2 ounces Jack Daniel's Tennessee Whiskey
1/2 ounce anisette
Dash of bitters

Combine all ingredients in a mixing glass with ice. Stir to chill. Strain into a chilled cocktail glass. Garnish with a black jelly bean and an orange twist.

ORANGE JACK MANHATTAN

★★★★★★★★★★★★★★★★★★★★★★★★★★★★

2 ounces Jack Daniel's Tennessee Whiskey
1 ounce orange curaçao
1 ounce fresh orange juice
Dash of bitters

Combine all ingredients in a mixing glass with ice. Stir to chill. Strain into a chilled cocktail glass. Garnish with an orange slice.

RED VELVET TENNESSEE MANHATTAN

★★★★★★★★★★★★★★★★★★★★★★★★★★★

2 ounces Jack Daniel's Tennessee Whiskey
2 ounces pomegranate juice
2 teaspoons simple syrup
Dash of bitters

Combine all ingredients in a mixing glass with ice. Stir to chill. Strain into a chilled cocktail glass. Garnish with a lemon twist.

TENNESSEE CHOCOLATE ALMOND MANHATTAN

★★★★★★★★★★★★★★★★★★★★★★★★★★★

2 ounces Jack Daniel's Tennessee Whiskey
1 ounce white créme de cacao
1/2 ounce amaretto

Combine all ingredients in a mixing glass with ice. Stir to chill. Strain into a chilled cocktail glass. Garnish with one whole almond (unsalted).

HEARD AROUND THE TABLE

I asked a couple in their thirties why they had chosen Miss Mary's for dinner that day. He said, "Today's our 7th anniversary, it is August 7th and we're visiting my favorite product, Old No. 7." Everyone clapped!

TENNESSEE CHOCOLATE MINT MANHATTAN

★★★★★★★★★★★★★★★★★★★★★★★★★

2 ounces Jack Daniel's Tennessee Whiskey
1 ounce white créme de cacao
1/2 ounce white créme de menthe

Combine all ingredients in a mixing glass with ice. Stir to chill. Strain into a chilled cocktail glass. Garnish with a floating fresh mint leaf.

GENTLEMAN'S SOUR APPLE MANHATTAN

★★★★★★★★★★★★★★★★★★★★★★★★★

2 ounces Gentleman Jack Rare Tennessee Whiskey
1 ounce sour mix
1 ounce apple schnapps

Combine all ingredients in a mixing glass with ice. Stir to chill. Strain into a chilled cocktail glass. Garnish with a thin slice of green apple.

JACK DANIEL'S OLD-FASHIONED

★★★★★★★★★★★★★★★★★★★★★★★★★

NOT REALLY A MANHATTAN and it's always served on the rocks, but the Old-Fashioned shares important classic status and I didn't know where else to put it!

1 orange slice
1 maraschino cherry
Dash of bitters
1 teaspoon superfine sugar
2 ounces Jack Daniel's Tennessee Whiskey

Muddle the orange slice, cherry, bitters, and sugar with a spoon in bottom of a rocks glass. Fill with ice. Top with Jack Daniel's. Add a splash of club soda if you like.

Nothing ruins a drink's first impression more than a badly cut garnish or one that's past its prime.

- **Citrus fruits**—For easy squeezing when you want the flavor of the juice in the drink, cut limes and lemons across in half through the fat middle and then cut each half into four chunks. Otherwise, cut festive wheels or half-wheels, or cut lengthwise into long thin wedges. Oranges are typically cut into thin half- or quarter-wheels.
- **Twist**—This is simply a thin slice of citrus rind, usually lemon or orange. You can buy a special tool or use a sharp paring knife. When zesting any citrus fruit, be sure to cut only deep enough to remove the colored peel without much of the bitter white pulp underneath. Twist the peel to release the oils and run it around the rim for flavor before dropping it in the drink.
- **Other Fruits**—Other interesting garnishes you can add to enhance or change the character of a drink (other than olives and onions) include thinly sliced green apple, fresh peach slices, pineapple chunks, star fruit, raspberries, blueberries, maraschino cherries, strawberries, melon balls, crystallized ginger, whole almonds, and even jelly beans and edible flowers. I prefer stemless maraschino cherries so as to not inconvenience my guests with an annoying "what do I do with this?" situation.

COMMON INGREDIENTS
garnishes

BACK IN UNCLE JACK'S day, whiskey was drunk neat followed with a chaser of cold water. He may have had lemonade, but probably not fresh ginger, pineapple, cranberry, apricot nectar, or even ginger ale. If he only knew how well his whiskey would blend with the flavors of the world, like green tea in China and maple syrup in Vermont!

HULA JACK

★★★★★★★★★★★★★★★★★★★★★★★★

1 teaspoon fresh grated ginger
1 teaspoon superfine sugar
Dash of bitters
2 ounces Jack Daniel's Tennessee Whiskey
1 ounce pineapple juice
4 ounces Sprite

Muddle ginger, sugar, and bitters with a spoon in the bottom of a tall glass. Fill with ice. Add Jack Daniel's and pineapple juice. Top with Sprite. Garnish with a lime wedge.

APRIJACK NECTAR

★★★★★★★★★★★★★★★★★★★★★★★★

1 1/2 ounces Jack Daniel's Tennessee Whiskey
3 ounces apricot nectar
1/2 ounce Rose's Lime Juice

Combine all ingredients over ice in a tall glass. Garnish with a lime wedge and mint sprig.

COCONUT ORANGE JACK

★★★★★★★★★★★★★★★★★★★★★★★★

2 ounces Jack Daniel's Tennessee Whiskey
1 ounce cream of coconut
3 ounces orange juice
Squeeze of fresh lime juice

Combine all ingredients in a shaker with ice. Shake vigorously. Pour into a tall glass. Or, combine all ingredients in the blender filled 1/3 full with ice. Blend until slushy. Garnish with an orange slice.

MADRAS JACKET

★★★★★★★★★★★★★★★★★★★★★★★★★★

2 ounces Jack Daniel's Tennessee Whiskey
2 ounces orange juice
2 ounces cranberry juice

Combine Jack Daniel's and orange juice over ice in a tall glass. Top with cranberry juice. Garnish with a lime wedge.

Glassware

Believe me, the glass is just as important as the drink it holds. That doesn't mean expensive, but you need the right glass for the drink *and* the occasion. Even when breaking the rules of glassware, the best bartenders stay true to the guiding principles and do it with confidence. I prefer clear glass to let the beautiful color of the cocktail shine through. The following glasses will do you nicely.

- **Rocks glasses**—A good rocks glass (also called the old-fashioned) is small and sturdy in the hand, perfect for sipping whiskey neat or over ice with a splash of water.
- **Highball**—This all-purpose glass can hold a good icy mixed drink like Jack and Coke. Get a few of the taller Collins glasses, perfect for Lynchburg Lemonade, if you have the space. Of course, we like to use chilled mason jars for fruity summer drinks with lots of ice.
- **Cocktail glasses**—If you don't have the shelf-space or patience for the V-shaped Manhattan-style up glass, serve strained chilled drinks in small wine glasses.
- **Wine glasses**—Stemmed ware shouldn't be confined to wines. I often serve an icy, fruity Jack mix in a stemmed glass for an especially elegant presentation. We used these for the Tomlyn Wedding Punch (see page 21) served at my wedding party.

JACK'S POMEGRANATE LEMONADE

★★★★★★★★★★★★★★★★★★★★★★★★★★

2 ounces Jack Daniel's Tennessee Whiskey
1 ounce pomegranate juice
Lemonade or Sprite

Combine Jack Daniel's and pomegranate juice over ice in a tall glass. Top with lemonade or Sprite. Garnish with a lemon wedge and mint sprig.

JACKARITA

★★★★★★★★★★★★★★★★★★★★★★★★★★

1 1/2 parts Jack Daniel's Tennessee Wiskey
1/2 part Triple Sec
3 parts margarita mix

Rub the rim of a cocktail glass with a lemon or lime slice and dip the glass rim in coarse salt. Shake the ingredients with ice and strain into the salt-rimmed glass.

JACK AND COKE

★★★★★★★★★★★★★★★★★★★★★★★★★★★★★★

2 ounces Jack Daniel's Tennessee Whiskey
Coke

Combine Jack and Coke over ice in a highball glass. Garnish with a lime wedge. You can also muddle a couple of lemon or lime wedges in the bottom of the glass. Add ice and Jack Daniel's. Top with Coke.

JACK AND COKE FLOAT
OR JACK BLACK COW

★★★★★★★★★★★★★★★★★★★★★★★★★★

Scoops of vanilla ice cream
2 ounces Jack Daniel's Tennessee Whiskey
Coke, root beer, or cream soda

Place a scoop or two of ice cream in a tall glass. Top with Jack Daniel's and your favorite soda. Serve with a spoon and a straw. Use whatever brown soda you like, even diet. I love a float made with root beer or cream soda. Talk about a fun afternoon sipper or casual dessert after a summer barbecue.

JACK ATTACK

★★★★★★★★★★★★★★★★★★★★★★★★★

2 ounces Jack Daniel's Tennessee Whiskey
Dash of bitters
Ginger ale

Combine all ingredients over ice in a tall glass. Garnish with a lime slice and a maraschino cherry.

THIS MAY BE THE MOST popular Jack Daniel's cocktail ever made. You'll find Jack and Coke served just about everywhere in the world. I like mine with a good healthy squeeze of fresh lime juice.

JACK AND SUN DROP

★★★★★★★★★★★★★★★★★★★★★★★★★

2 ounces Jack Daniel's Tennessee Whiskey
Sun Drop Citrus Soda

Pour Jack Daniel's in a tall glass with ice. Top with Sun Drop. Garnish with a lemon wedge.

SUN DROP HAS LONG been a local favorite. It's a yellow, really sweet lemon-lime soda that Lynchburg folks have been mixing for years. That must be why we're known for our sunny dispositions. It's not available everywhere so my cousin in South Carolina takes it home by the case after a visit.

FINISHING TOUCHES
to a Well-Served Cocktail

Little things matter, like festive beverage napkins and coasters. Paper napkins are fine as long as they are beverage-size, not dinner. I love my old-fashioned lacey cocktail napkins even though they need a little pressing. I want my guests to feel special because they are special. Spread around plenty of drink coasters so guests can set down their drinks without worry. As for drink stirrers, bartenders love them, but I find they're a nuisance and unnecessary, especially if you've properly mixed the drinks.

Long ago, Mother instilled in me the importance of a well-set table whether casual or formal. "Never just throw the silverware at the plates," she'd say. I like to accent a room with lots of candles and lower the lighting so everyone looks their best. On a cocktail buffet, arrange foods neatly and combine serving dishes of different heights and shapes.

CLASSIC JACK MINT JULEP
★★★★★★★★★★★★★★★★★★★★★★★★

Several sprigs of fresh mint (save one for garnish)
1 teaspoon superfine sugar
2 ounces Gentleman Jack Rare Tennessee Whiskey

Muddle mint sprigs with sugar in the bottom of a julep or rocks glass. Fill glass with crushed or cracked ice. Add Gentleman Jack. Garnish with a mint sprig.

PINEAPPLE JACK JULEP
★★★★★★★★★★★★★★★★★★★★★★★★

Several sprigs of fresh mint (save one for garnish)
1 teaspoon superfine sugar
1 1/2 ounces Jack Daniel's Tennessee Whiskey
2 ounces pineapple juice

Muddle mint sprigs with sugar in the bottom of a julep or rocks glass. Fill glass with crushed or cracked ice. Add remaining ingredients. Stir. Garnish with a mint sprig.

LEMON JACK JULEP
★★★★★★★★★★★★★★★★★★★★★★★★

Several sprigs of fresh mint (save one for garnish)
1 teaspoon superfine sugar
1 1/2 ounces Jack Daniel's Tennessee Whiskey
2 ounces fresh lemonade

Muddle mint sprigs with sugar in the bottom of a julep or rocks glass. Fill glass with crushed or cracked ice. Add remaining ingredients. Stir. Garnish with a mint sprig.

I'VE NOTICED A HEALTHY crop of fresh mint drinks growing like mad across the country. We've pulled up a few good ones that taste great all summer long. Legend has it that Uncle Jack made his juleps with tansy (now we know that tansy is toxic) instead of mint. The real secret is how to keep the specks of fresh mint out of your teeth. Be sure to try my other favorite juleps made with the Jack Daniel's fresh orange- or ginger-infused whiskies (see page 14).

a complementary flavor is called an infusion. Just combine fresh ginger or orange peel with a bottle of Jack Daniel's in a big jar and leave it be for about a week or so. You won't believe their delicious complexity. I've served these infusions as is over ice, in juleps, and blended with club soda, tonic, lemonade, ginger ale, or Sprite. Garnish the cocktails with orange slices, mint sprigs, or lime wedges. If you keep the infusions in a Jack Daniel's bottle, be sure to mark the bottle accordingly.

GINGER JACK

★★★★★★★★★★★★★★★★★★★★★★★★

2 hands ginger, peeled and coarsely chopped
1 bottle (750 ml) Jack Daniel's Tennessee Whiskey
1 cup sugar
1/2 cup water

Combine ginger and Jack Daniel's in a large jar. Store in a cool dark place for 1 to 2 weeks. Bring sugar and water to a boil and cook just until the sugar has dissolved. Cool. Strain the whiskey and discard the ginger. Stir syrup into the flavored whiskey. Store in a container with a tight-fitting lid.

ORANGE JACK

★★★★★★★★★★★★★★★★★★★★★★★★

4 or 5 large oranges
1 bottle (750 ml) Jack Daniel's Tennessee Whiskey
1 cup sugar
1/2 cup water

Using a sharp knife, cut the zest off the oranges in wide strips. Combine the zest and Jack Daniel's in a large jar. Store in a cool dark place for 1 to 2 weeks. Bring sugar and water to a boil and cook just until the sugar has dissolved. Cool. Strain the whiskey and discard the orange peel. Stir syrup into the flavored whiskey. Store in a container with a tight-fitting-lid.

CLASSIC TENNESSEE WHISKEY SOUR

★★★★★★★★★★★★★★★★★★★★★★★★★★

2 ounces Jack Daniel's Tennessee Whiskey
1 ounce fresh lemon juice
1 ounce simple syrup

Combine all ingredients in a shaker with ice. Shake vigorously. Strain and serve up in a sour glass or over ice in a highball glass. Garnish with an orange or lemon slice and a maraschino cherry.

PINEAPPLE JACK SOUR

★★★★★★★★★★★★★★★★★★★★★★★★

2 ounces Jack Daniel's Tennessee Whiskey
1 ounce Rose's Lime Juice
2 ounces pineapple juice

Combine all ingredients in a shaker with ice. Shake vigorously. Strain over ice in a highball glass. Garnish with a chunk of fresh pineapple and a maraschino cherry.

JACK JAJITO SOUR

★★★★★★★★★★★★★★★★★★★★★★★★

2 ounces Jack Daniel's Tennessee Whiskey
2 ounces fresh lime juice
1 ounce simple syrup
A few sprigs of fresh mint leaves, coarsely chopped

Combine all ingredients in a shaker with ice. Shake vigorously. Pour into a highball glass including the shaker ice and flecks of mint.

THE CLASSIC WHISKEY SOUR is a puckering blend of lightly sweetened lemon juice with whiskey garnished with a cherry and an orange slice. They need a good shaking to develop the characteristic foamy top. Serve the classic up in a sour glass or small wine glass or over ice in a highball. The others I prefer over ice. It's fun and easy to fiddle with the basic sour recipe and add a splash of another fresh juice and/or a dash of liqueur to complement the Jack. Here are a few of my favorites.

AT HOLIDAY TIME, WE don't do eggnog, we do boiled custard. I call ours "Bold" because that's certainly how it tastes when you add a little Jack. And a lot of us in Lynchburg pronounce the words "boiled" and "bold" virtually the same anyway, so why not? We wouldn't think of serving our holiday coconut or fruitcake without cups of boiled custard.

BOLD CUSTARD

★★★★★★★★★★★★★★★★★★★★★★★★★

1 quart whole milk or half-and-half
4 egg yolks
1/2 cup sugar
Pinch of salt
1 teaspoon vanilla
Whipped cream and nutmeg, optional
Jack Daniel's Tennessee Whiskey

Heat milk in a large saucepan over medium-low heat until it just begins to simmer. Beat egg yolks with sugar and salt in a small mixing bowl. Temper the egg yolks by gradually stirring in 1 cup of the hot milk. Pour egg mixture into the remaining hot milk in the saucepan. Cook over low heat, stirring constantly, until thickened and the custard coats the back of a wooden spoon. Do not allow to boil or the eggs will curdle and you'll have to start over. Cool. Stir in vanilla and chill before serving. Serve in small cups or glasses. Top with a dollop of whipped cream and/or a sprinkle of nutmeg, if desired. Pass a crystal pitcher of Jack Daniel's on the side for everyone to add as they please.
Makes 8 servings.

ALMOND JACK FROST

★★★★★★★★★★★★★★★★★★★★★★★★★

1 1/2 ounces Jack Daniel's Tennessee Whiskey
1/2 ounce amaretto
2 ounces cream
1 teaspoon superfine sugar

Combine all ingredients in a shaker with ice. Shake vigorously. Strain into a cocktail glass or serve over ice in a rocks glass. Sprinkle with nutmeg.

HOT TENNESSEE TODDY

★★★★★★★★★★★★★★★★★★★★★★★★★★

2 ounces Jack Daniel's Tennessee Whiskey
Spoonful of honey
Cinnamon stick
A good squeeze of fresh lemon juice
Boiling water

Pour Jack Daniel's into a mug. Add a spoonful of honey, cinnamon stick, and lemon juice. Top with boiling water and stir. Sit down. Relax. Enjoy.

HOT TOMATO JACK

★★★★★★★★★★★★★★★★★★★★★★★★★★

3 ounces tomato juice
3 ounces beef broth
2 ounces Jack Daniel's Tennessee Whiskey
Dash of Worcestershire sauce
Dash of hot pepper sauce
Squeeze of fresh lemon juice
Black pepper

Heat tomato juice and beef broth in a saucepan or microwave-safe mug. Stir in Jack Daniel's, Worcestershire sauce, hot pepper sauce, and lemon juice. Return to heat, if necessary. Serve in a mug. Sprinkle with black pepper and garnish with a lemon slice.

I'M NOT ALONE IN BELIEVING a warm Jack Daniel's toddy to be the best way to warm you up on a chilly day. Any of these potions are especially handy for cold weather tailgating. Mix one up and keep a warm batch ready in a thermos.

HEARD AROUND THE TABLE

While on the phone, I asked the man making the reservation if anyone in his party had trouble with steps. He replied "only after dinner."

JACK DANIEL'S WARM PEAR NECTAR SIPPER

★★★★★★★★★★★★★★★★★★★★★★★★

4 ounces hot pear nectar
2 ounces Jack Daniel's Tennessee Whiskey
1 tablespoon maple syrup

Combine all ingredients in a mug. Garnish with a sprinkle of nutmeg and a lemon slice.

HOT BUTTERED JACK

★★★★★★★★★★★★★★★★★★★★★★★★

2 ounces Jack Daniel's Tennessee Whiskey
1 teaspoon superfine sugar
Boiling water
Pat of butter

Pour Jack Daniel's in a mug. Top with boiling water. Stir in sugar. Top with a pat of butter. Garnish with a sprinkle of nutmeg.

HOT CHOCOLATE JACK

★★★★★★★★★★★★★★★★★★★★★★★★

2 ounces Jack Daniel's Tennessee Whiskey
5 ounces rich hot chocolate
Whipped cream

Combine Jack Daniel's and hot chocolate in a mug. Top with whipped cream. Garnish with a dusting of cinnamon or cocoa powder.

MULLED IN MOORE COUNTY

★★★★★★★★★★★★★★★★★★★★★★★★★★★

1 quart apple cider
1 cup orange juice
1 lemon, sliced
1 orange, sliced
1 stick cinnamon
2 teaspoons whole cloves
3 cups Jack Daniel's Tennessee Whiskey

Combine all ingredients except Jack Daniel's in a large pot. Simmer about 10 minutes for spices and juices to meld. Stir in Jack Daniel's and reheat. Serve in mugs. **Makes 16 servings.**

For a single serving—Place 2 ounces Jack Daniel's, a lemon slice, an orange slice, and cinnamon stick in a mug. Top with boiling apple cider.

COOL JACK APPLE MINT TEA

★★★★★★★★★★★★★★★★★★★★★★★★

1 part freshly brewed iced tea, sweetened to taste
2 parts apple cider
1 part Jack Daniel's Tennessee Whiskey
Green apple slices
Lemon slices
Mint sprigs

Combine all ingredients in a punch bowl or pitcher. Serve over ice.

TOLLEY TOWN CELEBRATION PUNCH

★★★★★★★★★★★★★★★★★★★★★★★★

4 parts cranberry juice
2 parts pineapple juice
1 part orange juice
3 parts Jack Daniel's Tennessee Whiskey
Fresh cranberries
Orange slices
Lemon slices

Combine all ingredients in a punch bowl or pitcher. Serve over ice.

Punch Bowls

I love Mother's old crystal and silver punch bowls with matching little cups, but they're not for every punch occasion. An overly "frou-frou" style can put a damper on some real fun, especially when gentlemen are present. Remember "punch" is simply a cocktail made in a larger batch. I like to be inventive and let the occasion choose the bowl. Big crocks and pottery bowls work great outdoors. Mismatched icy pitchers can look handsome in a group. Even big glass vases work well with a long-handled ladle. Just be sure whatever you choose is food safe and easy to wash.

JACK DANIEL'S CITRUS CIDER

★★★★★★★★★★★★★★★★★★★★★★★★★★

3 parts Jack Daniel's Tennessee Whiskey
2 parts apple cider
1 part orange juice
1 part lemon juice
4 parts ginger ale
Orange slices
Lemon slices
Green apple slices

Combine all ingredients in a punch bowl or pitcher. Serve over ice.
I make this festive punch in the fall when the air is crisp and cool.

TOMLYN WEDDING PUNCH

★★★★★★★★★★★★★★★★★★★★★★★★★

2 parts pineapple juice
1 part orange juice
1 part Jack Daniel's Tennessee Whiskey
1/4 part Rose's Lime Juice
Lime slices
Orange slices
Fresh mint sprigs

Combine all ingredients in a punch bowl or pitcher. Serve over ice.
We created this special punch for my wedding celebration held at the
Distillery Visitors Center. Add a little pomegranate juice to give it a
pinkish hue.

LYNCHBURG LEMONADE

★★★★★★★★★★★★★★★★★★★★★★★★★★★★★★

1 part Jack Daniel's Tennessee Whiskey
1 part Triple Sec
1 part bottled sweet-and-sour mix
4 parts Sprite
Lemon slices
Maraschino cherries

Combine all ingredients in a punch bowl or pitcher. Serve over ice.

TENNESSEE WHISKEY SOUR PUNCH

★★★★★★★★★★★★★★★★★★★★★★★★★★★★★★

1 can (12 ounces) frozen lemonade concentrate,
   undiluted and thawed
3 cans Jack Daniel's Tennessee Whiskey
2 cans orange juice
1 liter club soda
Orange slices
Lemon slices
Maraschino cherries

Pour lemonade concentrate into a punch bowl. Using the lemonade can, measure the Jack Daniel's and orange juice and pour into the punch bowl. Add club soda and fruit. Serve over ice. **Makes 16 servings.**

I do believe in a well-stocked bar. In fact, since I live in two places—Lynchburg during the week and Nashville on the weekends—I converted the laundry nook in my city townhome into a wet bar. My husband Tom teases me about it and loves to tell people "We have a lot of Jack Daniel's and a lot of dirty laundry!"

A well-stocked bar and a few simple tools are all you need for making great cocktails quickly. I keep my bar equipment together to avoid that exasperating last minute pre-party panic.

- **Shaker**—Cocktail shakers are fun and showy, but for me the Boston Shaker used by professional bartenders for shaking and stirring drinks works just fine. It's a stainless steel mixing/stirring cup on the bottom with a smaller glass that fits snugly in the steel half. Mix the drink with ice in the metal cup for stirring and shaking. Insert the glass top to cover tightly and shake. Let the cocktail mixture cool in the cold metal cup on ice for a moment. Then use a wire strainer to pour the drink into the glass leaving the ice behind. Some drinks don't require straining.
- **Wire strainer**—Place this over the mixing glass to strain a cocktail from the ice into a glass.
- **Stirring spoon**—A long-handled spoon comes in handy for stirring a drink in the tall mixing glass.
- **Reliable combination bottle and can opener**—When I was a little girl, Daddy called this a church key. I don't know what kind of church he was talking about, but I believe he attended regularly. You can find one that also has a good cork screw.
- **Small cutting board and sharp paring knife**—Small equipment is plenty adequate for cutting fruit garnishes. Don't fool with anything that's hard to store and takes up too much counter space.
- **Measuring cup and shot glass**—I use a little six-ounce glass that's really handy for measuring the whiskey and the mixers.
- **Towels and cleaning supplies**—No matter how tidy you are, bartending is sticky business. Keep things looking sharp with designated bar towels, paper towels, and a discreet bottle of bleach spray or all-purpose cleaner.

Our Nashville condo laundry bar that Tom keeps teasing me about. Yes, we do have a lot of Jack Daniel's and a lot of dirty laundry!

JACK HOUR
BITES

can stand a few spicy nuts to balance out happy hour. These party pecans are a nice little bit of everything—salty, sweet, savory, and spicy. I try to keep a bag or two in the freezer at all times for last-minute entertaining, hostess gifts, or grabbing a handful for Tom and me at about 5 p.m. Go ahead and double this recipe.

Helpful Hints for
COOKING WITH JACK

JACK'S SWEET HOT PARTY PECANS

★★★★★★★★★★★★★★★★★★★★★★★★★★

1/4 cup (1/2 stick) butter
3 tablespoons sugar
1/4 cup Jack Daniel's Tennessee Whiskey
2 tablespoons hot pepper sauce, or to taste
1 1/2 teaspoons salt
1/2 teaspoon garlic powder
4 cups (about 1 pound) pecan halves

Heat oven to 300°F. Combine all ingredients except pecans in large saucepan. Bring to a boil over medium heat, stirring to blend. Boil 3 minutes. Stir in pecans and toss well to coat. Spread nuts in a single layer in a jelly roll or roasting pan. Bake about 30 minutes or until nuts are crisp, stirring occasionally. Cool. Store in an airtight container. **Makes 4 cups.**

Conventional wisdom advises pairing robust flavored foods with big wines and spirits and vice versa. Well, not so with Jack. The unique quality of Jack Daniel's is that its sweet, spicy, woody, caramel flavor tastes equally delicious in hearty, flavorful foods like hickory-smoked barbecue as it does in delicate dishes like silky smooth custard.

Generally, when adding Jack to a recipe, allow enough time for the alcohol to mellow during heating. Many recipes call for bringing the liquid to a boil. This causes evaporation, but leaves Jack's lovely aroma and flavor.

Heating the spirit is not always necessary. Some dishes, like sweetened fresh fruits or dessert sauces, taste fabulous with a splash of Jack as is. Remember, a little goes a long way.

The golden rule (or the amber rule as we call it) of cooking with Jack is to show a little restraint. As with salt, pepper, cinnamon, or any other seasoning, moderation is always the key. The flavor of the Jack Daniel's should enhance and embrace a dish, not dominate it.

HOT CATFISH COCKTAIL SANDWICHES WITH YELLOW MUSTARD SLAW

★★★★★★★★★★★★★★★★★★★★★★★★★★★★

Vegetable oil
4 catfish fillets, cut into 2-inch pieces
1 cup self-rising cornmeal mix or plain cornmeal
   (season fish with salt, if using plain)
12 small, soft white dinner rolls
Yellow Mustard Slaw (see page 64)

Heat about 2 inches of oil in a cast-iron or heavy skillet to 365°F. Dredge catfish in cornmeal and let rest a few minutes to help the cornmeal adhere. Fry in hot oil until golden brown and crisp. Drain on paper towels. Place a piece of hot fish in a roll and top with a dollop of slaw. **Makes 12 servings.**

JACK'S RED DIPPING SAUCE

★★★★★★★★★★★★★★★★★★★★★★★★★★★★

1 1/2 cups ketchup
2 tablespoons brown sugar
1 to 2 tablespoons Worcestershire sauce
1 teaspoon dry mustard
1/3 cup Jack Daniel's Tennessee Whiskey
A few drops of hot pepper sauce or a spoonful of prepared horseradish,
   to taste

Combine ketchup, brown sugar, Worcestershire sauce, and dry mustard in a saucepan. Stir in the Jack Daniel's and simmer for 5 minutes, stirring occasionally. Refrigerate until serving time. Stir in hot pepper sauce or horseradish. Serve with fried catfish nuggets or cocktail wieners. **Makes about 2 cups.**

THE FRIED FISH SANDWICH is a hearty country staple, but it can easily be downsized into stylish cocktail fare. My Yellow Mustard Slaw has a tangier bite than the usual tartar sauce. Make sure the oil is good and hot before you start. Fry the catfish in several batches so you don't crowd the skillet and lower the oil temperature too much. Bite-size catfish nuggets served in little paper cones with Jack's Red Dipping Sauce (recipe follows) are also a party home run. You'll never go back to rubbery shrimp cocktail again!

AT MISS MARY'S WE DIP our fried catfish in this versatile sauce. Add a spoonful of fresh horseradish and serve it with chilled shrimp or cocktail catfish nuggets. And absolutely everyone loves this sauce warmed up with cocktail wieners.

FOR YEARS, I'VE experimented with every kind of trendy and time-honored appetizer, always searching for a new twist. In the end, absolutely nothing is more versatile, all-purpose, or delicious than pimiento cheese. We put it on everything—from plain old white bread to fancy crackers, in everything from celery stalks to Belgian endive spears—for any and all occasions. Do not take this simple spread for granted and please take care with your ingredients. Good pimiento cheese is not even a close cousin to the supermarket tubs of the overly sweet, dull orange spread. Good cheese, real mayonnaise, and quality pimientos are essential. Don't forget the secret ingredient—a pinch of sugar. For variety, I occasionally add a few chopped green or black olives.

LOOK NO FURTHER PIMIENTO CHEESE

★★★★★★★★★★★★★★★★★★★★★★★★★★

1/2 pound mild yellow cheddar cheese, grated (two cups)
1/2 pound sharp white cheddar cheese, grated (two cups)
Dash of Worcestershire sauce
Hot pepper sauce, to taste
1 jar (4 ounces) diced pimientos, with the juice
1/2 to 2/3 cup real mayonnaise
Pinch of sugar

Blend all ingredients together with a fork in a medium mixing bowl. Store covered in the refrigerator. **Makes about 4 cups.**

Back in the days before beautiful fresh red bell peppers were available all year long, jarred pimientos became the pantry staple for cooks looking to add a little color to casseroles and salads. They've earned a permanent place in most Southern pantries. Thank goodness for the genius who added the little red bits to shredded cheddar cheese and mayonnaise to make our traditional Southern sandwich spread—pimiento cheese!

The front of Miss Mary Bobo's Boarding House. Thousands of people have come in through these doors, but not a one ever left hungry!

HEARD AROUND THE TABLE

One day after dinner a guest asked me if I knew the name of the man standing by the front door. I told her he was the undertaker for a funeral home in nearby Fayetteville. She looked at me and asked, "What does he do, just hang around in case someone eats himself to death?"

everyone has a favorite cheese

CRISPY PECAN CHEESE WAFERS

★★★★★★★★★★★★★★★★★★★★★★★★

AROUND HERE JUST ABOUT
everyone has a favorite cheese wafer recipe. After more than 70 years of baking, Mother has declared this recipe *the best*. The crispy rice cereal adds an extra special crunch. You don't have to, but Mother adorns each wafer with a handsome pecan half that toasts while baking. When do we eat these? Every chance we get.

2 cups grated sharp cheddar cheese
1 cup (2 sticks) salted butter, softened
2 cups all-purpose flour
2 cups crispy rice cereal
Pinch of cayenne pepper
About 36 pecan halves

Heat oven to 375°F. Cream the cheese and butter in a large mixing bowl using an electric mixer. Slowly blend in the flour. Stir in the cereal and cayenne pepper. Drop batter by teaspoonfuls onto a cookie sheet and flatten out with the back of a spoon or a fork to make round wafers. Top each with a pecan half. Bake for 10 minutes or until just lightly browned. Cool on a wire rack. Store in an airtight container. **Makes about 36 wafers.**

TENNESSEE SMOKED TROUT SPREAD

★★★★★★★★★★★★★★★★★★★★★★★★

A LITTLE SEAFOOD NIBBLE is just the thing before a big steak or roast pork supper. Here I call for smoked trout, but you can substitute wood-smoked salmon with delicious results. Horseradish adds a tangy contrast to the smoky fish. Make the spread a day in advance so the flavors can mellow. I like it best with Melba toast or delicate water crackers.

1/3 cup grated fresh onion
1 tablespoon vegetable oil
2 tablespoons Jack Daniel's Tennessee Whiskey
Grated zest from 1 lemon
8 ounces smoked trout, skin removed, flaked into bite-size pieces
1/2 cup sour cream
2 tablespoons prepared horseradish
2 tablespoons chopped fresh parsley
2 teaspoons capers

CONTINUED ON NEXT PAGE

★★★★★★★★★★★★★★★★★★★★★★★★★★★★★★★★★★

Cook the onion in the oil in a small saucepan over medium heat until tender and lightly browned, about 3 minutes. Stir in the Jack Daniel's and lemon zest and cook until the liquid has evaporated, about 1 minute. Remove from heat and cool. Combine the trout, sour cream, and horseradish in a medium bowl and blend well. Stir in the onion mixture and remaining ingredients. Cover and refrigerate until serving time. Garnish with fresh lemon slices and additional parsley and capers. Serve with crackers. **Makes about 2 cups.**

THE REAL DEAL ONION DIP
★★★★★★★★★★★★★★★★★★★★★★★★★★★★★★★

6 to 8 slices bacon
3 cups chopped onion (about 3 medium or 2 large onions)
1 tablespoon sugar
1/3 cup Jack Daniel's Tennessee Whiskey
1 cup sour cream
1 cup yogurt
Salt and pepper, to taste
Hot pepper sauce, to taste

Cook the bacon in a large skillet until crisp. Remove the bacon, crumble, and set aside, leaving the drippings in the skillet. Cook onion in bacon drippings slowly over medium-low heat until lightly browned, about 20 minutes. Stir in the sugar and Jack Daniel's. Cook until all the liquid has evaporated, about 5 minutes. Spoon the onion mixture into a medium bowl and cool. Stir in the sour cream and yogurt. Add salt and pepper and a few dashes of hot pepper sauce. Store covered in the refrigerator. Sprinkle with bacon just before serving. Serve with chips, crackers, or raw vegetables. **Makes about 2 1/2 cups.**

THAT "DIP" THAT COMES in plastic tubs at the grocery store gives good old onion dip a bad rap. Make this one with sweet caramelized onions and smoky bacon and you'll find your tailgate parties will take on a much more sophisticated flavor. Colorful bell pepper strips make great dippers and I love those sturdy kettle-cooked potato chips.

THE COMBINATION OF pork sausage with ground beef makes these meatballs extra flavorful and moist. Mother and I are always on the lookout for locally made fresh pork sausage in the little country markets on the outskirts of town. Around here, farmers often process their own hogs and become real pork sausage experts, each with their own special seasoning blend. Apple butter adds body and a bit of sweetness to the meatball sauce, an old favorite on the Lynchburg party circuit. You can also serve the sauce with cocktail wieners, any kind of grilled pork, or even store-bought pulled pork barbecue.

SWEET HOT SOUR MASH MEATBALLS

★★★★★★★★★★★★★★★★★★★★★★★★

MEATBALLS
1 pound pork sausage
1 pound ground beef
1/2 cup plain dry bread crumbs
2 eggs, beaten
1/4 cup milk
1/2 cup finely chopped onion
1/2 teaspoon salt
1/2 teaspoon black pepper

APPLE BUTTER JACK SAUCE
3/4 cup spicy brown mustard
1/2 cup apple butter
1/3 cup Jack Daniel's Tennessee Whiskey
1/4 cup brown sugar
1 tablespoon cider vinegar
1 tablespoon Worcestershire sauce
Salt and black pepper, to taste
Hot pepper sauce, to taste

Heat oven to 375°F. Combine all the meatball ingredients in a large mixing bowl. Blend well with your hands. Form into 1 1/2-inch balls. Place them in an ungreased baking sheet (with sides to catch the grease) or on a jelly roll pan. Bake about 30 minutes or until browned and cooked through. Meatballs may be frozen and reheated at 350°F for about 20 minutes.

Combine all the sauce ingredients in a large skillet. Stir until well blended. Stir in cooked meatballs. Coat with sauce and cook about 5 minutes until sauce has thickened slightly. Serve with toothpicks.
Makes about 50 meatballs.

JACK BLACK BEAN DIP

★★★★★★★★★★★★★★★★★★★★★★★★★★

2 tablespoons vegetable oil

1 medium onion, chopped

2 cloves garlic, minced

2 cans (about 15 ounces each) black beans, drained

1/4 cup Jack Daniel's Tennessee Whiskey

1 teaspoon ground cumin

2 tablespoons fresh lemon juice

Hot pepper sauce, to taste

Suggested Toppings: sour cream, chopped avocado, chopped tomato, sliced green onions, and jalapeno peppers, chopped cilantro.

Heat oil in a large saucepan. Stir in onion and garlic and cook over medium heat until onions are tender, about 5 minutes. Stir in beans, Jack Daniel's, and cumin. Cook until bubbly and heated through. Mash beans lightly with a wooden spoon or a fork. Stir in lemon juice and hot pepper sauce. Serve warm or at room temperature in a serving dish topped with your choice of the suggested toppings. **Makes about 2 1/2 cups.**

Try making cheesy Mini Corncakes to serve with this dip. Use the recipe for Cast-Iron Cornbread (see page 48) and stir in a cup of grated sharp cheddar cheese. Simply drop spoonfuls of the batter on a hot greased griddle and cook just like regular little pancakes. Add a little more milk or water if the batter seems too thick. Mini Corncakes are also wonderful with pulled pork barbecue. Top the barbecue bites with a dollop of Clear Vinegar Slaw (see page 65).

WE SOUTHERN BEAN lovers raised on pintos, white beans, crowders, black-eyes, and limas are happy to welcome black beans to the family. Colorful toppings make this tasty dish a real standout, especially with chopped fresh summer tomatoes. Serve this dip with sturdy tortilla chips or Mini Corncakes.

as leftover deviled eggs. You certainly won't have any from this recipe, either. Sweet pickle relish is our secret. You may as well make more than you think you'll need because everyone eats at least one more than they really should. Garnish each egg with whatever you like. I've used sliced black or green olives, capers, fresh herbs like tiny fresh dill or parsley sprigs, a sliver of smoked salmon or country ham, crumbled crisp bacon, or just a dusting of paprika.

REALLY GOOD DEVILED EGGS

★★★★★★★★★★★★★★★★★★★★★★★

12 hard-cooked eggs, peeled and cut in half
1/2 cup mayonnaise
2 tablespoons yellow or Dijon mustard
1/3 cup sweet pickle relish
1/2 teaspoon salt and pepper, to taste
Dash of Worcestershire sauce
Hot pepper sauce, to taste

Remove the yolks from the egg whites and place the yolks in a medium bowl. Set the whites aside. Mash the yolks with a fork. Stir in the remaining ingredients until smooth. Spoon the yolk mixture into the egg whites and arrange on a platter. Garnish as desired. Cover and refrigerate. **Makes 24 halves.**

HOMETOWN HOT SALMON AND ARTICHOKE DIP

★★★★★★★★★★★★★★★★★★★★★★★★★★★★★★

1/4 cup (1/2 stick) plus 2 tablespoons butter

1/4 cup all-purpose flour

1 can (12 ounces) evaporated milk

2 tablespoon Jack Daniel's Tennessee Whiskey

1 teaspoon Worcestershire sauce

1 teaspoon paprika

1/2 teaspoon garlic salt

Black pepper, to taste

2 cans (6 ounces) salmon without bones

1 can (about 14 ounces) artichoke hearts, drained and coarsely chopped

1 tablespoon lemon juice

1/2 cup cracker crumbs

1/3 cup grated Parmesan cheese

1/3 cup chopped fresh parsley

Heat oven to 400°F. Grease a 1 1/2-quart shallow baking dish. Melt 1/4 cup of the butter in a large saucepan over medium heat. Blend in the flour until smooth. Cook, stirring constantly, until bubbly, about 1 to 2 minutes. Stir in the evaporated milk. Cook until thickened and bubbly. Stir in Jack Daniel's, Worcestershire sauce, paprika, garlic salt, and pepper. Fold in salmon, artichoke hearts, and lemon juice. Pour into the greased baking dish. Combine cracker crumbs, Parmesan cheese, and parsley in a small bowl. Sprinkle over the casserole. Dot with remaining two tablespoons of butter. Bake 30 minutes or until lightly browned and bubbly. Garnish with lemon slices. Serve warm with fancy crackers or Melba toast. **Makes 10 to 12 servings.**

ARTICHOKE DIP HAS gotten so popular, it just doesn't seem special like it used to. Because this is filling and fun to scoop, guests appreciate small cocktail plates so they can double dip with abandon. If it's just heavy hors d'oeuvres for dinner, I always plan to serve at least one special warm dish along with the usual fruits, vegetables, and cheeses. Add a small can of black olives to the salmon mixture if you like.

life's greatest pleasures and I cannot imagine living in a world without them. One of my all-time favorites is hand-cut home-made French fries. We cook big batches of fries in a turkey fryer outside and serve them with this cool trio of dipping sauces. Natural-cut frozen fries save time and are almost just as good as long as they're fried, not oven baked. Try these versatile sauces with other fried snacks like chicken wings or tenders or any fried vegetables.

PEPPERY JACK BLUE CHEESE DIPPING SAUCE

★★★★★★★★★★★★★★★★★★★★★★★★

1 cup mayonnaise
1/2 cup sour cream
1 cup (4 ounces) crumbled blue cheese
1/4 teaspoon garlic powder
1 teaspoon Worcestershire sauce
2 tablespoons Jack Daniel's Tennessee Whiskey
Hot pepper sauce, to taste

Combine all ingredients in a medium bowl. Blend well. Cover and keep refrigerated. **Makes about 2 1/2 cups.**

HOT MUSTARD JACK DIPPING SAUCE

★★★★★★★★★★★★★★★★★★★★★★★★

1 cup coarse-grained mustard
1 cup mayonnaise
1/4 cup Jack Daniel's Tennessee Whiskey
1/4 cup honey
Hot pepper sauce, to taste

Combine all ingredients in a medium bowl. Blend well. Cover and keep refrigerated. **Makes about 2 1/2 cups.**

TENNESSEE/LOUISIANA BORDER DIPPING SAUCE

★★★★★★★★★★★★★★★★★★★★★★★★★★★★

2 cups ketchup
1/4 cup brown sugar
3 tablespoons Worcestershire sauce
1/2 cup Jack Daniel's Tennessee Whiskey
Hot pepper sauce, to taste

Combine all ingredients in a small saucepan. Bring to a boil and simmer 2 to 3 minutes. Cool. Cover and keep refrigerated. **Makes about 2 1/2 cups.**

HEARD AROUND THE TABLE

A lady from France called for reservations and directions to Miss Mary's. I told her to come to the town square and look for the gazebo on the corner. Turn at the gazebo and we're the third house on the left. When she arrived she told me that she thought I had said *casino* on the phone, not *gazebo*. She looked everywhere for the casino!

JACKGRITA SIPPERS

★★★★★★★★★★★★★★★★★★★★★★★★★★

1 cup tomato juice
1 cup orange juice
1/2 cup lime juice
1/2 cup Jack Daniel's Tennessee Whiskey
2 tablespoons pomegranate juice
2 tablespoons sugar
Hot pepper sauce, to taste

Combine all ingredients in a pitcher. Chill and serve in shot glasses.
Garnish with fresh cilantro sprigs. **Makes 12 servings.**

PEACHY JACK SIPPERS

★★★★★★★★★★★★★★★★★★★★★★★★★★

4 cups sliced, peeled fresh peaches (or 4 cups frozen peach slices)
1 1/2 cups orange juice
1/4 cup lime juice
1 tablespoon sugar, or more to taste
1/2 cup Jack Daniel's Tennessee Whiskey
1 teaspoon almond extract

Puree peaches in a blender with the orange and lime juices and sugar.
Stir in Jack Daniel's and almond extract. Chill in a pitcher and serve in
shot glasses. Garnish with mint sprigs. **Makes 12 servings.**

THESE THREE-SIP "SOUPS"
are a perfect party conversation
starter and have been known to
bring even the dullest guests to life.
Pass the sippers on a tray as you
greet and mingle with your guests
and in no time, everyone will ask
for the recipe—and another sip.

Can't you see the family resemblance? This bronze statue stands at the entrance to the Cave Spring, our source of iron-free water for making Jack Daniel's Tennessee Whiskey.

TENNESSEE LEMON DROP SIPPERS

★★★★★★★★★★★★★★★★★★★★★★★★★

1 pint Italian Lemon Ice or lemon sherbet
Jack Daniel's Tennessee Whiskey

Fill shot glasses with a small scoop of lemon ice. Top with Jack Daniel's. Garnish with mint sprigs. Sip as the lemon ice melts into the whiskey. Try this with other sorbet flavors like peach mango or raspberry. **Makes 12 servings.**

JACK OYSTER SLURPS

★★★★★★★★★★★★★★★★★★★★★★★★★

Freshly shucked oysters
Jack Daniel's Tennessee Whiskey
Hot pepper sauce
Fresh lemon wedges

Shuck a fresh oyster and place in a shot glass. Top with a drizzle of Jack Daniel's, dash of hot pepper sauce, and a squeeze of fresh lemon juice. **Makes 1 slurp per oyster.**

We have fabulous fresh tomatoes and a long growing season in Middle Tennessee thanks to the mild weather and the limey soil. The Bradley is our crown jewel with its pinkish skin and sweet flavor. Often we're still eating fresh ripe tomatoes all the way to Halloween! Then it's time to get the green tomatoes in the skillet.

COMMON INGREDIENTS

Tennessee Tomatoes

MOTHER'S VEGETABLE PARTY SANDWICHES

★★★★★★★★★★★★★★★★★★★★★★★★★★

1 package (8 ounces) cream cheese
2 medium carrots
1 small green or red bell pepper
1 medium cucumber
1 small onion
Mayonnaise, to taste
Salt, to taste
Prepared horseradish or hot pepper sauce, to taste
24 slices thin-sliced white bread

Allow cream cheese to soften at room temperature. Grate the vegetables on the fine side of a grater. Allow to sit a few minutes and be sure to drain very well. Blend vegetables with cream cheese, adding enough mayonnaise to make a nice spreadable mixture. Stir in salt and horseradish. Spread on bread and top with another slice. Cut off crusts and cut into four squares or fingers. **Makes about 4 dozen finger sandwiches.**

TOM'S TOMATO SANDWICHES

★★★★★★★★★★★★★★★★★★★★★★★★★★

I don't know who loves tomatoes more—Mother or my husband Tom. Naturally, they both love them with bacon. Use good white bread, sliced ripe tomatoes, crisp bacon, and plenty of real mayonnaise. Make them small for a party or big for supper.

YEARS AGO WHEN MOTHER was active in bridge club, the competition for the finest lunch spread (and the cleanest house) was fierce in her circle. One time Daddy came home to find Mother and Dee scrubbing the chimney before the gals arrived and declared they had simply gone too far! The house was spotless and Mother upped the ante with these to-die-for party sandwiches. Even today, Mother's friends expect her to bring plenty of them to gatherings. She finds them especially spirit-lifting after a funeral.

wings is a favorite snack before ball games and barbecues. Since smoking pork butts is an all-day affair, and whole hog an all-night one, the Lynchburg barbecue fellas grill up piles of chicken wings to snack on while they "work." After grilling the wings, they'll toss them in a big foil pan of special whiskey hot sauce and pass it around. They don't seem to bother much with the blue cheese dressing and I can't say I've ever seen anyone munching on the carrot and celery sticks, either. Serve them anyway for folks like me who need a little cooling balance for the wings.

JACK HOT WINGS

★★★★★★★★★★★★★★★★★★★★★★★★★

CHICKEN

3/4 cup all-purpose flour
1 1/2 teaspoons salt
1/4 teaspoon black pepper
2 pounds chicken drumettes
Vegetable oil

SAUCE

1/2 cup (1 stick) butter
1/2 cup Jack Daniel's Tennessee Whiskey
1/4 cup ketchup
1/3 cup hot pepper sauce, or to taste

Combine flour, salt, and pepper in a shallow bowl. Coat the wings with the flour mixture. Heat 2 to 3 inches of oil in a fryer or heavy pot to 365°F. Fry wings, a few at a time, until golden brown on all sides and cooked through, about 10 to 15 minutes. Drain on paper towels.

Combine all the sauce ingredients in a small saucepan. Bring to a boil. Dip cooked wings in the sauce. Serve with blue cheese dressing and fresh celery and carrot sticks. **Makes 6 to 8 servings.**

To bake the wings, place them in a roasting pan. Brush wings with melted butter and sprinkle with salt and pepper. Bake in a 450°F oven until lightly browned and cooked through, about 30 minutes. Don't forget you can grill the wings over medium heat for about 30 minutes, turning frequently.

Folks ask all the time about my Uncle Jack. Jasper Newton Daniel was a runaway at age six, a distiller by age thirteen, and a remarkable innovator his whole life. Apparently, he was a real character.

At six, with his mother dead, nine siblings at home, and his father newly married, Jack left the family. I guess he just wasn't getting enough attention. He came to live with the Call family, headed by a Lutheran minister and whiskey maker, Dan Call. Mr. Call taught Jack how to make whiskey and even made him a partner in the operation. Call eventually sold the business to Uncle Jack after deciding to devote more time to his ministry.

Jack moved the distillery to a source of limestone water flowing from the Cave Spring in Lynchburg. The cold water ran at a constant fifty-six degrees and was free of good whiskey's worst enemy, iron. He was the first to register his distillery during the early 1860s when the federal government began the regulation and taxation of whiskey.

Quite an astute businessman, Jack sold his whiskey to both sides during the Civil War, a risky proposition at the time. Just as we do today, he also held true to the charcoal-mellowing process when other whiskey makers opted for quicker, cheaper methods after the war. Charcoal mellowing made his whiskey more expensive, but gave it a unique smooth character, enough that the U.S. Government specially designated it as "Tennessee Whiskey," not bourbon.

Uncle Jack was a small man, standing only five feet-two inches tall, but hardheaded about making charcoal-mellowed Tennessee Whiskey. When other whiskey makers opted for round bottles, he chose square. Jack Daniel came to world attention at the 1904 St. Louis World's Fair and Centennial Exposition. He traveled to the fair by train and returned four days later with the World's Fair Gold Medal for the best whiskey in the world. This was the first of seven gold medals his Old No. 7 whiskey would earn.

The story goes that it was his temper that killed him. One day he had trouble with the combination on his office safe and, out of frustration, gave it a good swift kick. At first, he only suffered a limp, but gangrene eventually set in and six years later, on October 10, 1911, Jack Daniel died. He's buried in Lynchburg Cemetery on the hill just above the town square.

Because Uncle Jack never married, the Distillery passed to his nephew Lem Motlow whose name still appears in the fine print on every bottle of Jack Daniel's Tennessee Whiskey. Lem was responsible for seeing the Distillery through the difficult twenty-nine years of Federal and State Prohibition. When Prohibition ended in Tennessee, he reopened the Distillery and revived the charcoal-mellowing tradition.

Jasper Newton (Jack) Daniel

BREADS & BREAKFAST

biscuits is handling the dough just enough. Not too much kneading, but enough so the dough holds together and makes nice flakey layers. I roll out my biscuits quite thin, about 1/2-inch thick if I'm planning to make country ham biscuits. Big fluffy biscuits may be more to your liking for breakfast. Roll those out about 3/4-inch thick. Make them with any size cutter you like or none at all and cut the dough into rough squares. For cocktail parties, I prefer tiny two-bite biscuits. You'll need a little more liquid if using buttermilk.

COMMON
INGREDIENTS

self-rising flour and cornmeal mix

HOMEMADE BISCUITS

★★★★★★★★★★★★★★★★★★★★★★★★★★★

1/3 cup lard or vegetable shortening
2 cups self-rising flour
3/4 cup milk or almost 1 cup buttermilk

Heat oven to 450°F. Cut the lard into flour with a pastry blender or two knives until the mixture looks like coarse crumbs. Add milk and stir just until a soft dough forms. Turn dough out onto a lightly floured surface or pastry cloth. Knead gently just until smooth, about 10 times. Roll out or pat out the dough with your fingers to about 1/2- to 3/4-inch thickness. Cut into rounds with a floured (2-inch) biscuit cutter. Place on a baking sheet. Bake 10 to 12 minutes or until golden brown. Brush melted butter on the biscuit tops right when they come out of the oven.
Makes about 12 biscuits.

To use all-purpose flour in a recipe that calls for self-rising, add 1 1/2 teaspoons baking powder and 1/4 teaspoon of salt per cup of flour.

These have been a regular grocery store item in the South since the days when rural Southerners baked everyday. These modern inventions made life easier by premixing the salt and leavening in the right amounts for biscuits and cornbread. We also use the flour and cornmeal for anything that requires salt, like dredging meats, fish, and vegetables for frying.

HEARD AROUND THE TABLE

A Swiss boy thought sausage biscuits were hamburgers.

SOUTHERN CORNBREAD IS

all about the crust. It's crisp on the outside and moist, never dry, on the inside. Anyone who says they don't like cornbread hasn't had any good cornbread. Unlike other parts of the country, we use white cornmeal, we don't add sugar (or not much anyway) and the recipe is mostly cornmeal, not half cornmeal and half flour. Use any size cast-iron skillet you want, but Mother and I like it best in a large one so the bread is thin and crusty. If you don't have a good cast-iron skillet, then get one! Flip the cornbread out of the pan and serve crusty brown-side up. You can use this same recipe for griddle corncakes, muffins, or corn sticks. Keep leftovers in the freezer and you're ready to make cornbread dressing anytime.

CAST-IRON CORNBREAD

★★★★★★★★★★★★★★★★★★★★★★★★★★

1 egg
1/4 cup bacon drippings or vegetable oil
2 cups self-rising cornmeal mix
About 1 1/3 cups milk or 1 3/4 cups buttermilk

Heat the oven to 450°F. Grease a 9-, 10-, or 12-inch cast-iron skillet and place it in the oven to get good and hot. Combine egg and oil in a medium mixing bowl and blend well. Stir in the cornmeal mix and milk until smooth and creamy. The batter should be pourable like pancake batter. If it seems a little thick, add a little more milk or water. Pour the batter into the hot skillet and bake until the crust is golden brown. The 9-inch skillet will take about 20 to 25 minutes to bake, the large skillet will take about 15 to 18 minutes to bake and the medium skillet will take somewhere in between. **Makes 8 servings.**

Self-rising cornmeal mix is an everyday item to us here in Lynchburg and across the South. If you can't find it, then try 1 3/4 cups plain white or yellow cornmeal blended with 1/4 cup of all-purpose flour, 2 1/2 teaspoons of baking powder, and 1/2 teaspoon salt.

Add one or some of these to the basic cornbread recipe:

1 cup shredded cheddar or Jack cheese
1/2 cup crumbled bacon, pork cracklings, or diced country ham
1 cup crumbled cooked sausage
1 small can or 2 chopped green chilies
1 small can cream-style corn
1/2 cup sautéed onions and diced green bell peppers
1/2 cup sugar (Don't even think about it!)

Maggie makes corn muffins in our well seasoned pans. Notice the batter isn't too thick and is easy to pour. That's the secret to moist cornbread.

SOUTHERN SPOON ROLLS

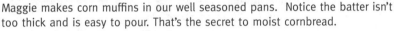

1 package active dry yeast
2 cups warm water
1/2 cup sugar
1/2 cup (1 stick) butter, melted
1 egg, beaten
4 cups self-rising flour

Grease 24 muffin cups. Combine yeast and warm water in a large mixing bowl and stir until the yeast has dissolved. Stir in the sugar, butter, and egg. Add the flour, stirring vigorously until a soft dough forms, about 2 minutes. At this point, you can cover and refrigerate the dough overnight and then bake the rolls the next day. Or, loosely cover the mixing bowl and let the dough rest on the countertop for about 20 minutes. Drop by spoonfuls into muffin cups. Bake at 400°F for 15 to 20 minutes or until golden brown. Brush the hot rolls with additional melted butter and serve immediately. **Makes about 24 rolls.**

THE SOUTH HAS A LONG tradition of soft, white warm breads. I once brought Mother a dozen delicious authentic chewy bagels from New York City. She gave them a good try but declared bagels much too chewy and cold for her! We serve these soft yeast rolls at Miss Mary's whenever cornbread or biscuits don't already have a place on the menu.

WE GET MORE REQUESTS
at Miss Mary's for this simple recipe than even for our mashed potatoes! Frozen hash browns and canned soup may not sound fancy, but you can't argue with the result. Keep this recipe handy for entertaining because you can't beat creamy, cheesy potatoes with just about any chicken, red meat, or pork dish. And don't forget them on the sideboard for brunch. Stir in a small jar of pimientos for color. We often turn it into a main dish by adding chopped baked ham, country ham, cooked and crumbled pork sausage, Italian sausage or Kielbasa. Cooked spinach, sautéed red and green peppers, and even a handful of corn kernels are colorful easy add-ins.

IRON SKILLET SEASONING

HASH BROWN POTATO BAKE

★★★★★★★★★★★★★★★★★★★★★★★★★★

1 medium onion, chopped
1/2 cup butter
1 bag (30 ounces) frozen hash brown potatoes, thawed
1 1/2 cups sour cream
2 cups (8 ounces) grated sharp cheddar cheese
1 can (10.75 ounces) condensed cream of mushroom soup

Heat oven to 350°F. Grease a 9 x 13-inch baking dish. Cook the onion in the butter in a medium skillet over medium heat until tender, about 5 minutes. Combine the remaining ingredients in a large mixing bowl and blend well. Stir in the onions and butter. Pour the mixture into the greased baking dish. Bake about 1 hour or until golden brown and hot. Garnish with a sprinkling of fresh parsley. **Makes about 12 servings.**

Few utensils are as important in the Southern kitchen as a good iron skillet for frying meats and developing the all-important crispy cornbread crust. Cast iron requires regular, but simple care to develop its natural nonstick finish.

Here's how to make and keep a skillet slick: Clean new, unseasoned, or rusty cast-iron cookware with soapy hot water and a stiff brush. Sometimes I use steel wool if the pan is rusty. Dry completely. Spread a thin layer of vegetable oil or shortening on all surfaces. Heat the cookware upside down in the oven

at 350°F for about an hour. Place a sheet of foil on the rack below to keep the oven clean.

Always clean your seasoned-cast iron with hot water and a brush, never with soap or harsh detergent (and never in the dishwasher). Dry thoroughly to prevent rust. Fry as much bacon, sausage, and chicken as possible. Your cornbread will never stick.

MUFFIN CUP HAM BISCUITS

★★★★★★★★★★★★★★★★★★★★★★★★★★

2 cups self-rising flour
1 cup milk
1/2 cup mayonnaise
2 cups chopped country ham

Heat oven to 425°F. Grease 12 regular or 24 mini muffin cups. Combine all the ingredients in a large mixing bowl. Stir with a fork to make a soft dough. Drop by spoonfuls into the greased muffin cups. Bake until golden brown, about 15 minutes for regular, or 8 to 10 minutes for mini muffins. **Makes 12 regular size or 24 mini muffins.**

DEBBIE BAXTER, THE assistant manager at Miss Mary's, often stirs up batches of these Muffin Cup Ham Biscuits for a big weekend breakfast. Debbie likes that they're easier than rolled-out biscuits and they have terrific country ham flavor. You can also make them with a pound of cooked and crumbed pork sausage instead of the country ham. There's nothing better with a pot of grits and fried eggs. These muffins reheat well so she keeps some in the freezer for a quick weekday breakfast for her husband Goose and daughter Rebecca. Mayonnaise replaces the usual shortening and creates a cake-like texture and rich flavor. As ever, a bag of country ham scraps in the freezer is sure convenient for recipes like this. When I have a cocktail party in Nashville, my city friends love a mini cocktail version with their Jack and a splash.

GAME DAY SWEET POTATO MUFFINS

★★★★★★★★★★★★★★★★★★★★★★★★

1 1/2 cups self-rising flour
3/4 cup plus 2 tablespoons sugar
1 teaspoon cinnamon
1/4 teaspoon nutmeg
1/4 teaspoon ginger
1/3 cup vegetable oil
2 eggs, beaten
2 tablespoons Jack Daniel's Tennessee Whiskey, optional
1 cup mashed cooked sweet potato or pumpkin puree
1/2 cup chopped toasted pecans

Heat oven to 375°F. Grease 12 muffin cups or 24 mini muffin cups. Combine flour, 3/4 cup of the sugar, cinnamon, and nutmeg in a large mixing bowl and blend well. Stir in oil, eggs, Jack Daniel's, and sweet potatoes until well blended. Spoon into muffin cups. Sprinkle with pecans and remaining sugar. Bake 15 to 20 minutes for regular size muffins, 10 to 13 minutes for mini muffins.
Makes 12 regular or 24 mini muffins.

SOME OF THE MOST elaborate cooking I've ever seen has been performed in crowded parking lots on game day. When it's my turn, I go for finger foods, good sandwiches and a crock of steaming soup. These moist mini sweet potato or pumpkin muffins are an annual fall tailgate favorite that pack and travel exceptionally well. Add a drop or two of Jack Daniel's to the batter for fun.

TIMS FORD HUSH PUPPIES

★★★★★★★★★★★★★★★★★★★★★★★★★★

2 cups self-rising cornmeal mix
2 tablespoons self-rising flour
2 tablespoons brown sugar
2 tablespoons finely chopped onion
2 tablespoons finely chopped green bell pepper
1 cup milk
2 eggs, beaten
Vegetable oil for frying

Combine cornmeal, flour, sugar, onion, and green pepper in a medium mixing bowl. Stir in milk and eggs and blend well. Set aside for 5 minutes; do not stir. Drop by small spoonfuls in hot (365°F) oil. Fry until golden brown. Drain on paper towels. **Makes about 20 hush puppies.**

WHY ANYONE WOULD TAKE the time to fry fish without making a side of hush puppies is beyond me. A good hush puppy is always deep golden brown, crisp and light in the center and never greasy. They're best eaten right out of the fryer. Cold ones are only fit for the dogs! Here we break our own rule against sugar in cornbread by adding just a little brown sugar to the batter. We named these hush puppies after Tims Ford Lake, a favorite of our local fishermen for bluegill, small and largemouth bass, catfish, and crappie.

visit Miss Mary's have never had the opportunity to try good Southern grits. The mere mention of this strange sounding word elicits jeers or fears from the uninitiated. Grits are nothing more than coarsely ground corn cooked in liquid and seasoned. Even we sometimes forget that grits do more than just soak up red-eye gravy and sunny-side up eggs. A good cheese grits casserole is as versatile as macaroni and cheese or potatoes au gratin. We love them for breakfast or dinner. Though the homely name often confines grits to country cooking, they can be quite sophisticated. Experiment with other good cheeses like Swiss, goat, or Parmesan and always add plenty of butter.

COMMON
INGREDIENTS
grits

CHEESE GRITS BAKE

★★★★★★★★★★★★★★★★★★★★★★★★★★

4 cups water
1 teaspoon salt
1 cup quick cooking grits
1/4 cup (1/2 stick) butter
2 1/2 cups grated Cheddar cheese, divided
1 cup milk
4 eggs, beaten
1 clove garlic, minced
1 tablespoon Worcestershire sauce
Dash of hot pepper sauce

Heat oven to 350°F. Grease a 9 x 13-inch baking dish. Combine water and salt in a large saucepan. Bring to a boil. Stir in the grits. Reduce heat to low, cover, and cook until thickened, about 5 minutes. Remove from heat and stir in the butter and 2 cups of the cheese until melted. Stir in the milk, eggs, garlic, Worcestershire sauce, and hot pepper sauce. Pour into the greased baking dish. Sprinkle with the remaining 1/2 cup of cheese. Bake 45 minutes or until golden brown. **Makes 10 servings.**

Grits are simply coarsely ground corn cooked in water until creamy and soft. You'll most often find them ground from white corn, but yellow is also available. We like them best for breakfast with plenty of salt, pepper, and butter. Their versatile mild flavor makes them easy to pair and combine with all kinds of foods like cheeses, vegetables, and meats.

SUNDAY SAUSAGE SPINACH STRATA

★★★★★★★★★★★★★★★★★★★★★★★★★★★★

12 slices good quality white bread, crust removed if you like
1 pound cooked and crumbled pork sausage
1 package (10 ounces) frozen spinach, thawed and squeezed dry
1 can (14.5 ounces) diced tomatoes, drained
1/2 teaspoon garlic powder
3 cups grated sharp cheddar cheese, divided
2 1/2 cups milk
6 eggs
1/2 teaspoon salt
Black pepper, to taste

Grease a 9 x 13-inch baking dish. Place 6 slices of the bread in the bottom of the dish. Top the bread evenly with sausage, spinach, and tomatoes. Sprinkle with garlic powder and 1 1/2 cups of the cheese. Top with the remaining 6 slices of bread. Combine milk and eggs in a medium bowl. Whisk until well blended. Pour over the bread. Top with the remaining 1 1/2 cups of cheese. Cover and refrigerate at least 6 hours or overnight. Heat oven to 350°F and bake uncovered 50 to 60 minutes or until golden brown and puffy. **Makes 8 servings.**

for Tom and me. We're usually traveling between our Lynchburg country home and our big city weekend pied-á-terre in Nashville. We often travel separately so the cars are where we need them. Thank goodness for books on tape and this make-ahead eggy casserole. Because strata requires a few hours of soaking and sitting in the refrigerator, most folks prepare it the night before for an easy bake-and-serve brunch. I make it Sunday morning to bake for supper, wherever we end up.

HEARD AROUND THE TABLE

A cautious gentleman from Australia agreed to try *one* grit.

their coffee, family and guests will insist on seconds of this rich cake that's appropriate for breakfast, brunch, an afternoon indulgence, or late night snack. Make this recipe once and I guarantee this page will be dog-eared for all-time. Mindy makes it with apples and, of course, Mother insists on tossing in a handful of chopped fresh cranberries, too.

APPLE CRISP COFFEE CAKE

★★★★★★★★★★★★★★★★★★★★★★★★★

CRISP TOPPING

1 cup chopped pecans
3/4 cup all-purpose flour
3/4 cup brown sugar
1/2 cup (1 stick) butter, melted
1/2 teaspoon cinnamon
1/4 teaspoon salt

CAKE

2 cups self-rising flour
1 1/2 cups sugar
1/2 cup (1 stick) butter, melted
1 cup sour cream
3 eggs, beaten
2 teaspoons vanilla
2 Granny Smith or Golden Delicious apples, peeled, cored, and diced

Heat oven to 350°F. Grease a 9 x 13-inch baking pan. Combine all the Crisp Topping ingredients in a mixing bowl with a fork until crumbly. Set aside.

Combine flour and sugar in a large mixing bowl. Stir in butter, sour cream, eggs, and vanilla until smooth. Pour into the greased pan. Sprinkle with apples, then the Crisp Topping. Bake 30 to 45 minutes or until toothpick inserted in the center comes out clean. Serve warm or at room temperature. **Makes 16 servings.**

PAN-DRIPPINGS GRAVY

★★★★★★★★★★★★★★★★★★★★★★★★

1/4 cup pan drippings and browned bits from frying meat
1/4 cup all-purpose flour
2 to 3 cups liquid (milk or broth)
Salt and pepper, to taste

Leave 1/4 cup of fat and the browned bits in a skillet after frying meat or poultry. Stir in flour with a fork to blend well. Cook over medium heat for about 1 minute. Gradually stir in the liquid. Bring the mixture to a boil, stirring constantly. Cook until thickened, about 2 to 3 minutes. Season with salt and pepper. **Makes 2 to 3 cups.**

RED-EYE GRAVY

★★★★★★★★★★★★★★★★★★★★★★★★

Drippings from frying country ham
Water
Pinch of sugar

After frying country ham, add water to the skillet and scrape up the browned bits from the bottom. Add a pinch of sugar. It's supposed to be thin and watery. Serve with country ham.

IF THERE'S MEAT FRYING in a Southern skillet, chances are good we'll be making gravy with the drippings and the biscuits will already be in the oven. Whether for pork chops, steak, chicken, sausage, or squirrel, our gravies are as important to country cooking as the Mother sauces are to France. The only rule is to use equal parts pan drippings to flour. The amount of liquid depends on how thick you like your gravy. I use all milk for sausage gravy and a combination of milk and broth for chicken gravy. Red-eye gravy made with country ham drippings isn't thickened at all. We prefer all water, but some folks I know add a little black coffee.

crust is perfect for my pastry-challenged big brother, Jimmy Lee, (at home we still call him by both names, everyone else calls him Lee). I'm very fond of him and his manly quiche despite Dee's confession to Mother when I was born that she'd never love me like her sweet little Jimmy Lee. Like the rest of the Tolley family, he's quite comfortable in the kitchen and does most of the cooking at his house. Lee's wife Pat relaxes with the Sunday paper while he whips up this special breakfast pie.

JIMMY LEE'S WEEKEND BREAKFAST PIE

★★★★★★★★★★★★★★★★★★★★★★★★

1 1/2 cups cracker crumbs (about 1 sleeve of crackers)
1/2 cup (1 stick) melted butter
6 slices bacon
1 cup chopped onion
1 cup sour cream
3 eggs
1/2 teaspoon salt
2 cups shredded Swiss or Monterey Jack cheese
1/2 cup shredded sharp cheddar cheese

Heat the oven to 375°F. Combine cracker crumbs and butter in a small bowl. Press the crumbs into a 9-inch pie plate. Cook bacon in a skillet over medium heat until crisp. Remove bacon and crumble into a mixing bowl. Cook onion in the skillet with the drippings over medium heat until tender. Add onions to the bacon. Stir in sour cream, eggs, and salt and blend well with a fork. Stir in the Swiss cheese and pour the mixture into the pie plate. Sprinkle the top with cheddar cheese. Bake 25 to 30 minutes or until set. **Makes 6 to 8 servings.**

My brother Jimmy Lee and me as kids on the front porch playing cowboys. I'm sure this display of affection was Mother's idea.

A man from California told about his first experience with grits at a truck stop where he had ordered ham and eggs. He had his eye on the big pot of white stuff that the cook kept stirring. When the waitress brought him his plate, he said, "This isn't my order because I didn't order that white stuff." She replied, "Honey, those are grits and nobody orders them but everybody gets them!" He was ashamed to ask about the reddish liquid in the small bowl. Finally, he asked the man sitting beside him who told him it was red-eye gravy: "What do I put it on?" "Everything!" the man replied.

The oldest part of Miss Mary Bobo's Boarding House has been around since the 1820s. Back in those days folks built homes right over a source of water if they could. To this day, a natural spring runs under the back of the house even though we're on the city water now. The front of the house was added in the 1850s. Miss Mary and her husband Jack bought the building in 1908 and she boarded guests there until her death in 1983, just shy of 102 years old. Until a hip injury slowed Miss Mary down at 98, she had actively managed her boarding house, supervising cooks, servers, and gardeners, buying groceries, paying bills, and greeting her guests at the front door.

Most of Miss Mary's boarders were single school teachers, traveling salesmen, and the United States tax revenue agents who were assigned to the Distillery. Tom Motlow (the brother of Lem Motlow who inherited the Distillery from Uncle Jack) was a confirmed old bachelor and president of the Farmers Bank. He lived at the house until his death at age 96. The gregarious leg-puller Roger Brashears, who ran the Distillery Visitors Center for years and is still Lynchburg's most colorful storyteller, lived in the house during his younger days in the late 1960s and early '70s. He laughs now that he weighed 182 pounds when he moved in and 287 pounds when he moved out six years later.

Mary Ruth Hall, a Moore County extension home economist, was also a boarder. She moved to Lynchburg in 1949 and paid $12.50 a week for room, board, and three meals a day. This was one-fourth of her salary and she had a good government job right after the war. In her retirement years, Miss Mary Ruth was a popular table hostess at Miss Mary's.

And then there is Leola Dismukes, my second mother. Dill, or Dee Dee as we called her, took care of my brother, Jimmy Lee, and me when we were children. Later on, she cooked for Miss Mary for nearly twenty-five years beginning in the mid-1960s. I guess after Lee and I moved away to school, Dee needed new mouths to feed. She is our most loved family friend.

When Miss Mary passed away, her children were in their seventies and not interested in running the property. When the house went for sale, folks in town were concerned that the Boarding House would close or, worse, be torn down. Thankfully, the Distillery purchased Miss Mary's from her children and pre-

Miss Mary Bobo

served its place in our rich history. I was hired to take over as proprietress and we reopened on May 1, 1984. We've been busy serving noonday dinner ever since. I figure I'll last until I reach 102 since I'm eating the same wholesome foods that Miss Mary did.

MISS MARY BOBO'S BOARDING HOUSE
Today

I have enjoyed running Miss Mary Bobo's Boarding House since it re-opened as a restaurant in 1984. We haven't boarded guests for years, but we still prepare and serve home-cooked, family-style meals with friendly Southern hospitality.

Midday dinner at Miss Mary's is steeped in tradition. Folks gather together on the front porch and in the yard under the big maple trees, introduce themselves, and visit. We ring a prompt dinner bell and call each party's name to one of our five family-style tables. A Lynchburg hostess attends to each table, leading introductions, encouraging conversation, and instructing on passing protocol. Our only rule is this: serve yourself from the dish in front of you and always pass to the left. Don't worry about getting enough to eat here. Just like Miss Mary, we keep the bowls and casseroles filled so there's plenty for everyone.

What's on our dinner menu? Well, it does depend on the day you visit, but every meal includes two meats, six country-style vegetables and side dishes, freshly brewed iced tea, cornbread or rolls, and a delicious homemade dessert with coffee. Being a dry county since 1909, of course, we can't serve you Mr. Jack's product in a glass. That doesn't mean we can't slip some into your dinner!

Some of our best-loved dishes are loved best thanks to that special, not-so-secret ingredient.

When we're not serving our year-end holiday meal, our menu includes favorites like these:

- Miss Mary's Chicken with Pastry
- Skillet Fried Chicken
- Tender Pork Roast
- Crispy Fried Catfish
- Lynchburg Candied Apples (every single day)
- Squash Casserole
- Speckled Butter Beans with Sweet Pepper Relish
- Cabbage Casserole
- Carrot Casserole
- Real Mashed Potatoes
- Turnip Greens
- Country-Style Green Beans with Fresh Tomato Relish
- Superlative Fried Okra (every single day)
- Slaw
- Carrot Raisin Salad

SALADS & SOUPS

THREE STYLES OF SLAW

There isn't one slaw that can do it all, but I believe three just might. This Yellow Mustard Slaw is my version of the one served on the slaw burgers at Honey's Pool Room on the town square in nearby Fayetteville. It's also real good on grilled hot dogs and sausages. The White Mayo Slaw is the creamy one, dressed with a simple combination of mayo, vinegar, and sugar. I love it with catfish. The Clear Vinegar Slaw is my first choice to serve with real hickory-smoked barbecue ribs or pulled pork, perfect for cutting through the fat. You just don't need a lot of creamy mayo with rich meat. We use finely grated cabbage so that the slaw sits nicely atop a pulled pork sandwich. Add other vegetables to any of these green cabbage-based slaws for any occasion. Try bell pepper, carrots, red cabbage, or sliced celery. Tart chopped apple adds another interesting dimension.

YELLOW MUSTARD SLAW
★★★★★★★★★★★★★★★★★★★★★★★★★★

1/4 cup grated (about 1 medium) onion
1/4 cup sugar
1/4 cup cider vinegar
1/4 cup sweet pickle relish
1/4 cup prepared yellow mustard
1/2 teaspoon salt
1/2 teaspoon celery seed
Hot pepper sauce, to taste
16 ounces (about 8 cups) finely shredded cabbage or packaged slaw mix

Combine onion, sugar, vinegar, pickle relish, mustard, salt, celery seed, and hot pepper sauce in a small bowl. Blend well. Pour dressing over the cabbage in a large bowl. Stir thoroughly. The more you stir, the more the cabbage packs down and the saucier it gets. Serve it good and cold. **Makes 8 servings.**

WHITE MAYO SLAW

★★★★★★★★★★★★★★★★★★★★★★★★★★★

1/4 cup mayonnaise

1/4 cup cider vinegar

1/4 cup sugar

1/2 teaspoon salt

1/2 teaspoon celery seed, optional

16 ounces (about 8 cups) finely shredded cabbage or packaged
    slaw mix

Combine mayonnaise, vinegar, sugar, salt, and celery seed in a small
bowl. Blend well. Pour dressing over the cabbage in a large bowl. Stir
thoroughly. Keep refrigerated until serving. Make the mustard or vinegar
slaws if you're going to a hot summer picnic. **Makes 8 servings.**

CLEAR VINEGAR SLAW

★★★★★★★★★★★★★★★★★★★★★★★★★★★

1/2 cup cider vinegar

1/2 cup sugar

1/2 cup water

1 teaspoon salt

16 ounces (about 8 cups) grated or finely shredded cabbage
    or packaged slaw mix

Combine vinegar, sugar, water, and salt in a small bowl. Blend well, but
don't worry that the sugar hasn't dissolved completely. Pour dressing
over the cabbage in a large bowl. Stir thoroughly. Serve it good and cold.
Makes 8 servings.

to do with big creamy soft lima beans. Baby limas and butter peas have a fresh texture and taste when cooked until just tender. We can buy already shucked beans at farm stands in the late summer, but the frozen ones work just as well. The tender little beans hold their shape when tossed with rice, colorful vegetables, and the tangy vinaigrette. Made without sour cream or mayonnaise, this salad is ideal for a hot summer picnic or supper outside. Make it a few hours or a day ahead to allow time for the flavors to meld.

BABY LIMA RICE SALAD

★★★★★★★★★★★★★★★★★★★★★★★★★

16 ounces frozen baby limas, cooked until just tender,
   drained and cooled
1 1/2 cups cooked rice
1 cup sliced celery
1 cup shredded red cabbage
1/2 cup chopped parsley
1/3 cup chopped red onion
1/2 cup olive oil
2 tablespoons Dijon mustard
2 tablespoons fresh lemon juice
1 small clove garlic, finely minced and mashed into a paste
Salt and pepper, to taste
Cherry tomatoes, cut in half

Combine beans, rice, celery, red cabbage, parsley, and onion in a large bowl. To make the dressing, combine olive oil, mustard, lemon juice, and garlic in a small bowl. Blend well with a fork. Stir the dressing into the vegetables. Season with salt and pepper. Garnish with cherry tomatoes.
Makes 8 servings.

BABY SPINACH AND BEETS WITH HOG JOWL DRESSING

★★★★★★★★★★★★★★★★★★★★★★★★★★

1 pound baby spinach
1 can (14.5 ounces) sliced beets, drained
6 slices hog jowl or bacon
1 medium Vidalia onion, chopped
2 teaspoons sugar
3 tablespoons cider vinegar
2 tablespoons Jack Daniel's Tennessee Whiskey
Salt and pepper, to taste
Croutons

Combine spinach and beets in a salad bowl. Cook hog jowl in a skillet over medium heat until crisp. Remove, cool, and crumble. Add onion and sugar to the drippings in the skillet and cook until the onion is softened. Stir in the vinegar and Jack Daniel's. Cook and stir until slightly thickened. Pour over spinach and beets. Season with salt and pepper and toss. Sprinkle with crumbled hog jowl and croutons. Serve immediately. **Makes 8 servings.**

EVERYTHING IS BETTER with bacon (and Jack Daniel's), even beets. Our favorite "bacon" is actually hog jowl that we can buy sliced by the pound. Mother prefers it because it's more consistent. "You never know about bacon," she says. "Sometimes you get a good package, others aren't worth a thing." Canned beets are convenient, but fresh ones roasted in the oven or in a foil packet on the grill are even better.

with a little Jack Daniel's is a marvelous complement to fresh fruits. The flavor is rich, but doesn't overpower the fruit. Don't worry if you're lacking a fruit or two called for in the recipe. Mix it up with what's in season and what's in the refrigerator crisper drawer. We love a handful of miniature marshmallows thrown in and even occasionally some toasted chopped pecans.

COUNTRY CITRUS FRUIT SALAD

★★★★★★★★★★★★★★★★★★★★★★★★★

3 seedless oranges, peeled and cut into bite-size chunks
1 small pineapple, cut into 1-inch cubes
2 firm, but ripe bananas, sliced
1 medium bunch of red seedless grapes
1 pint fresh strawberries, halved
3/4 cup brown sugar, or to taste
1/4 cup Jack Daniel's Tennessee Whiskey
1/2 cup shredded coconut
1 cup chopped Toasted Pecans, optional (recipe follows)

Combine all the fruits in a large bowl. Combine sugar and Jack Daniel's in a small bowl. Blend well. Gently stir mixture into the fruit. Sprinkle with coconut and pecans. **Makes 8 servings.**

Southern fruit salads, congealed or not, are often creamy, very sweet and can be served for dessert. Here's a simple fruit salad you'll find at Miss Mary's. Combine 8 ounces of cream cheese with about 1/4 cup of heavy cream and blend until fluffy. Stir in a good old can of drained fruit cocktail and some drained crushed pineapple. Chill and serve.

TOASTED PECANS

★★★★★★★★★★★★★★★★★★★★★★★★★

Toasted pecans make all the difference in many of our recipes. To toast nuts, place them in a dry skillet over medium-low heat, stirring frequently, about 5 minutes. When you begin to smell their aroma, the nuts are ready. Toast extra and keep them in the freezer. Many guests comment on our carrot raisin salad thanks to the toasted pecans. Our traditional recipe contains the usual grated carrots, crushed pineapple, shredded coconut, mayonnaise and, of course, lots of sugar. Toasted chopped pecans give the salad an earthy taste that beautifully ties it all together.

HEARD AROUND THE TABLE

At a delicatessen in Cleveland, Ohio, where I was picking up a few things, the young girl waiting on me shyly inquired, "May I ask what nationality you are?" I was so flabbergasted that I asked her, "What nationality do you think I am?" "Australian," she replied. I said "Not quite that far South, Honey!"

We ring the bell every day before dinner, but it doesn't take much to get everyone's attention.

of home cooks went wild over congealed salads. Hardworking homemakers considered them a modern miracle for adding color and fun to the rural Southern table. The explosion of readily available canned fruits and vegetables encouraged congealed creativity in every shade of color and texture. Sweet, savory, creamy, or tart, we had them all the time with everything. This adults-only salad inspired by one of our favorite cocktails will have you reconsidering this time-honored tradition. Be sure to zest the lemon before squeezing the juice.

LYNCHBURG LEMONADE CONGEALED SALAD

★★★★★★★★★★★★★★★★★★★★★★★★

2 packets (4 1/2 teaspoons) unflavored gelatin
1/3 cup Jack Daniel's Tennessee Whiskey
1 1/2 cups boiling water
3/4 cups sugar
Zest from 1 fresh lemon
1/2 cup fresh lemon juice
1 cup orange juice
1 can (15.4 ounces) crushed pineapple in juice
2 cups miniature marshmallows
1 cup chopped toasted pecans

Sprinkle gelatin over Jack Daniel's in a medium bowl to soften. Let stand about 5 minutes. Add boiling water, sugar, and lemon zest. Stir until sugar and gelatin are completely dissolved, about 1 minute. Add lemon and orange juices. Chill in a 2-quart casserole or bowl until slightly thickened. Stir in pineapple, marshmallows, and pecans. Cover and chill until firm. Garnish with orange slices. **Makes 8 servings.**

CREAMY SHOEPEG CORN SALAD

★★★★★★★★★★★★★★★★★★★★★★★★★★★★★

3 cups cooked and cooled shoepeg corn (you'll need 2 packages, 10
    ounces each, frozen corn)
1 small green bell pepper, chopped
1/4 cup chopped red onion
1/2 cup sour cream
1 tablespoon mayonnaise
1 tablespoon vinegar
1/4 teaspoon celery salt
Pinch of sugar
Salt and pepper to taste

Combine all ingredients in a medium bowl. Blend well. Cover and
refrigerate until serving time. **Makes 8 servings.**

CREAMY ENGLISH PEA SALAD

★★★★★★★★★★★★★★★★★★★★★★★★★★★★★

3 cups frozen green peas, cooked until just tender and cooled
    (1 16-ounce bag)
1/2 cup sliced celery
1/2 cup chopped red bell pepper
1/4 cup chopped red onion
1/2 cup sour cream
1 tablespoon mayonnaise
1/4 cup celery salt
Pinch of sugar

Combine all ingredients in a medium bowl. Blend well. Cover and
refrigerate until serving time. **Makes 8 servings.**

CREAMY SHOEPEG CORN Salad and Creamy English Pea Salad are Southern classics and favorites at Miss Mary's. Both are dressed with a blend of sour cream and mayonnaise and the all-important pinch of sugar. Serve either one when a leafy green salad just won't do, like for covered dish suppers, picnics, and buffet sideboards.

White, sweet shoepeg is our favorite corn. The small elongated kernels resemble the small pegs used to attach soles to boots back in the 1800s.

AT MISS MARY'S WE OFTEN make English Pea Salad with frozen peas and pearl onions and omit the red onion. Don't bother with mushy canned peas. Instead, cook frozen peas just a couple of minutes to retain their gorgeous green color and fresh texture. Feel free to use a small jar of diced pimiento instead of the red bell pepper. I've also enjoyed many pea salad variations that include chopped hard-boiled egg and diced cheddar cheese.

You can plan and plan and cook forever, but if host and guest don't do their parts, good food and drink can't save an occasion. At Miss Mary's, each table is led by a seasoned hostess who does her best to ensure a good time for all. Simply put, a good hostess uses good manners and common sense. Keep our simple approach in mind for all gatherings.

- **Introductions break the ice.** We ask each guest to introduce themselves before we begin the meal. Conversation comes easier when you know a first name and hometown. Suddenly, there's plenty to talk about.
- **Talk up the menu.** We want our guests to appreciate the specially chosen menu. You will at your party, too. As the bowls are passed to the left, we talk a little about each dish and encourage generous helpings. At home I do the same, taking care to point out the bar and share highlights of the buffet or dinner.
- **Get conversation rolling.** Be prepared to ask lots of good questions and help your guests find common ground among themselves. Our table hostesses keep a few funny stories and local lore in mind to jump start a quiet table. Good listening makes better conversation.
- **Go with the flow.** A seasoned hostess expects the unexpected. Even at Miss Mary's we've weathered plenty of dinner dilemmas with a laugh and a smile. Your good guests will be ready to jump in and help.

PLAN A VISIT TO
Miss Mary Bobo's Boarding House

In rural Tennessee, we call the midday meal "dinner"—not lunch—and in the evening we eat "supper." Just as in Uncle Jack's day, we serve dinner family-style Monday through Saturday

Reservations are a must so most folks call us well in advance of their visit. We sure don't want to turn you away so please call ahead. (Try not to call between 11 a.m. and 2 p.m. CST time while we're fixing and hosting dinner.) Closed on Sunday and all major holidays.

Miss Mary Bobo's Boarding House
Lynchburg, Tennessee, USA 37352
(931) 759-7394

Our table hostesses keep the conversation lively and the dishes passing to the left. That day I was lucky to host visitors from Australia, Romania, Pennsylvania, and nearby Portland, Tennessee.

Besides experiencing one of the best country-style dinners you might ever taste, I guarantee you'll revel in the company of your table companions. Our guests hail from every state and nearly every country in the world. One month, we served dinner to friends from forty-three states and seventeen countries! On any day you could have a couple from Brazil on your right and a family from rural Minnesota on your left. We may come to the table as strangers, but we'll leave as friends.

are a recent arrival in the South. Growing up, the only time we enjoyed lettuce was when the baby greens came up in the spring garden along with the radishes and green onions. Mother would toss together a big batch of this salad wilted with plenty of salty sweet bacon dressing. We loved it so much that on occasion it was all she'd fix for supper.

LYNNE'S FAVORITE SALAD DRESSINGS

EARLY SPRING GREENS WITH WARM BACON DRESSING

★★★★★★★★★★★★★★★★★★★★★★★★★★★★

1 pound baby lettuce, rinsed and dried
8 green onions, sliced
10 radishes, thinly sliced
8 slices bacon
1/4 cup cider vinegar
1 tablespoon sugar
Salt and pepper, to taste
2 hard-boiled eggs, chopped

Toss lettuce, onions, and radishes in a large salad bowl. Cook bacon in a large skillet over medium heat until crisp. Remove and crumble the bacon; set aside. Remove all but 1/4 cup of the bacon drippings from the skillet. Stir in the vinegar and sugar. Cook over medium heat until the sugar has dissolved. Pour warm dressing over the salad and toss. Season with salt and pepper. Top with crumbled bacon and eggs. **Makes 6 servings.**

When iceberg lettuce came along, we began to enjoy leafy garden salads more often like our urban cousins. As a child, I could never have imagined the fancy greens tossed in salad bowls nowadays. I still enjoy a fat icy cold wedge of iceberg with any of my favorite creamy dressings and a sprinkling of crisp bacon sure doesn't hurt. Mother and I also still treat ourselves to chilled canned pears with a little dab of Thousand Island. Use the classic vinaigrette on more delicate greens.

THOUSAND ISLAND DRESSING

★★★★★★★★★★★★★★★★★★★★★★★★★★

1 cup mayonnaise

1/3 cup chili sauce

1/3 cup sweet pickle relish

1 tablespoon fresh lemon juice

Salt and pepper, to taste

Combine all ingredients in a small bowl. Cover and chill until serving time. **Makes about 2 cups.**

CREAMY HERB DRESSING

★★★★★★★★★★★★★★★★★★★★★★★★★★

1 clove garlic, finely minced and mashed into a paste

1/2 cup mayonnaise

1/2 cup buttermilk

2 tablespoons fresh lemon juice

2 tablespoons minced fresh parsley

2 tablespoons minced fresh chives

Dash of Worcestershire sauce

Salt and pepper, to taste

Combine all ingredients in a small bowl. You can also use other fresh herbs like thyme and oregano. Cover and chill until serving time. **Makes about 1 1/2cups.**

BLUE CHEESE DRESSING

★★★★★★★★★★★★★★★★★★★★★★★★★★

1/2 cup mayonnaise
1/2 cup buttermilk
1/2 cup crumbled blue cheese
Dash of Worcestershire sauce
1 tablespoon fresh lemon juice
1/4 teaspoon garlic powder
1/4 teaspoon dried oregano
Salt and pepper, to taste

Combine all ingredients in a small bowl. Cover and chill until serving time. **Makes about 1 1/2 cups.**

DIJON VINAIGRETTE

★★★★★★★★★★★★★★★★★★★★★★★★★★

1 small clove garlic, minced and mashed into a paste
1/3 cup wine vinegar
1 teaspoon Dijon mustard
1 cup olive oil
Salt and pepper, to taste

Combine all ingredients in a small bowl. Whisk until well blended. Toss on salad greens or cover and store in the refrigerator.
Makes about 1 1/2 cups.

A healthy crop of watercress grows on the banks of the little creek that meanders just behind Miss Mary's. I love it with Dijon Vinagrette or simply dressed with olive oil, a squeeze of lemon juice, and a sprinkling of salt. Its peppery crunch and tangy lemon flavor makes a perfect bed for a pile of freshly fried catfish nuggets.

CRANBERRY FRUIT FLUFF

★★★★★★★★★★★★★★★★★★★★★★★★★★★★★★

2 cups fresh cranberries, ground in a food processor
3 cups miniature marshmallows
3/4 cup sugar
2 crisp apples, cored and diced
1/2 cup seedless green or red grapes, cut in half
1/2 cup toasted pecans or walnuts
Pinch of salt
1 cup heavy cream, whipped

Combine cranberries, marshmallows, and sugar in a mixing bowl. Cover and chill overnight. Stir in apples, grapes, nuts, and salt. (Feel free to experiment with other fruits in season.) Fold in whipped cream and chill before serving. **Makes 8 servings.**

MOTHER LOVES CRANBERRIES so much she's likely to add them to almost anything and not just during the holiday season. In fact, she was delighted the time I ordered way too many fresh cranberries for Miss Mary's. Mother rescued the extras and stashed them in freezer bags to use all year long. This old favorite is like a showy cousin of the Waldorf salad. It's a gorgeous pink color, fluffy, and decadent. Mother insists on the overnight rest for the cranberries, marshmallows, and sugar. The next day, the marshmallows have nearly disappeared into the creamy mix. And no, we don't eat it for dessert. It's a salad!

DEBBIE BAXTER'S PARENTS, David and Ola Cleek, have been making sauerkraut from homegrown Firm Flat Dutch Cabbage Heads (they say the hybrid cabbage just doesn't work) since Debbie was a child. The age-old process of brining and preserving cabbage packed in canning jars takes 30 to 60 days. Even now the grown children fight over the tender cabbage stalks that her mother inserts in the center of each jar. The Cleeks tend a big vegetable garden and luckily Debbie's husband Goose likes to do the same (although she says he works her to death). It doesn't take long in the spring for the family competition over "who's got what in the garden and how big is it" heats up. "Daddy calls Goose all the time to boast about the first corn, cabbage, beans, or tomatoes they're having for supper. 'Have you had that yet?' he'll gloat." Kraut salad is another Miss Mary's favorite even though it often seems a little unusual to many of our guests. Surprisingly good, the crisp texture and sweet/sour flavor is a first-rate match for pork.

CRISPY KRAUT SALAD

★★★★★★★★★★★★★★★★★★★★★★★★

4 cups sauerkraut, rinsed and drained
1 cup sliced celery
1/2 cup chopped green bell pepper
1/2 cup chopped red bell pepper
1/2 cup chopped red onion
1 cup sugar
1 cup vinegar
1/4 cup vegetable oil
Salt and pepper, to taste

Combine all ingredients in a large bowl. Serve well chilled.
Makes 8 servings.

Debbie and Goose love their vegetable garden. As usual, here's Goose telling Debbie what to do. Thanks to Debbie, our guests enjoy fresh zinnias at Miss Mary's all summer long.

LEFTOVERS BAKED POTATO SOUP

★★★★★★★★★★★★★★★★★★★★★★★★★★★★★★★★★

4 large baking potatoes, baked and cooled
2/3 cup (11 tablespoons) butter
2/3 cup all-purpose flour
6 cups milk
Salt and pepper, to taste
4 green onions, sliced
1/4 cup crumbled cooked bacon
1 1/2 cups shredded cheddar cheese
1/2 cup sour cream

Cut potatoes in half, scoop out the insides, and set aside. Discard the skins. Melt the butter in a Dutch oven or large pot. Stir in flour until smooth. Cook over medium heat, stirring constantly, until bubbly and golden, about 1 to 2 minutes. Gradually add the milk. Cook over medium heat until thickened and bubbly. Stir in the potatoes, salt and pepper, half the sliced onions, bacon, and 1 cup of the cheese. Cook until heated through and cheese is melted. Stir in sour cream. Add extra milk if the soup seems too thick. Serve individual portions topped with a sprinkling of the remaining cheese and green onions. **Makes 8 servings.**

WE LOVE LEFTOVERS Baked Potato Soup on cold days, which is why in wintertime we often throw extra potatoes in the oven so we'll have some "leftovers." Other cooked vegetables and meats are fun to add as well. Stir in a cup or so of corn, bits of country ham, grilled chicken, even green beans.

combines three Southern classics in one dish—white beans, country ham, and greens. The only thing missing is the cornbread! Serve a bowl of chowchow or red pepper relish on the table. Some of us like a dash of hot pepper sauce, as well.

WHITE BEAN SOUP WITH COUNTRY HAM AND GREENS

★★★★★★★★★★★★★★★★★★★★★★★★★

1 pound white beans, picked over and soaked overnight
2 tablespoons oil
2 medium onions, chopped
6 ounces country ham, diced
3 cloves garlic, minced
1 bay leaf
2 cans (14 ounces each) chicken broth
1/2 pound turnip or mustard greens, collards or kale, tough stems removed and greens cut into 1-inch strips

Drain the soaked beans. Cook onion in oil in a large soup pot until tender. Stir in the country ham and garlic and continue to cook for another minute or two. Add beans, bay leaf, chicken broth, and enough water to cover. Simmer about 1 to 1 1/2 hours or until the beans are tender. Add additional water during simmering if the beans seem too thick. Add the greens to the beans and simmer just until the greens are tender, about 10 minutes. Season to taste with salt and pepper.
Makes 10 servings.

TENNESSEE ONION SOUP

★★★★★★★★★★★★★★★★★★★★★★★★★★

2 tablespoons butter
2 tablespoons oil
6 cups sliced onions
1/2 cup Jack Daniel's Tennessee Whiskey
1 tablespoon sugar
6 cups beef broth
1/4 teaspoon dried thyme
Salt and pepper, to taste
8 slices toasted French bread, cut into bite-size chunks
2 cups grated Monterey Jack or hickory smoked cheddar cheese

Heat butter and oil in a Dutch oven or soup pot. Cook onions over low heat, stirring occasionally, until a rich brown color, about 20 minutes. Stir in the Jack Daniel's and sugar and continue to cook a few more minutes. Stir in the broth and thyme. Simmer 15 to 20 minutes. Season with salt and pepper. Top each serving with French bread and about 1/4 cup grated cheese. If using oven-proof soup crocks, run them under the broiler for just a moment to melt the cheese. **Makes 8 servings.**

WHEN COLD WINTER winds are whipping through the hollow, Tom and I like nothing better than a hot bowl of Tennessee Onion Soup. A splash of the home-town product and a crown of melted Jack or hickory-smoked Cheddar makes this our very own version of the famous French classic. Don't make the mistake of cooking the onions too quickly. It takes time for the natural sugars to caramelize and develop a nutty sweet flavor.

With nearly two dozen varieties of inexpensive, nutritious peas and beans available, our tables are seldom without one kind or another served as a side, a salad, a soup, or even as a main dish. White beans, pintos, and black-eyed peas are on the top of our list. We also cook a wide variety of limas and others in the pea family, like crowders, lady and field peas. Whether fresh, frozen, or dried, we cook them all the same—in a big pot simmered and flavored with cured pork, the other vital Southern ingredient.

COMMON
INGREDIENTS
beans

GOOSE BAXTER,
a seasoned tour guide at the Distillery and avid hunter, says squirrel hunting is a lazy man's sport because you don't go anywhere. "Find yourself a hickory, beech, or white oak tree where they're feeding on the nuts. Go lean up on nearby tree and wait. We call it still hunting because you sit real still." Sounds good to me—just relaxing and enjoying the scenery. Squirrel hunters like Goose enjoy a big fried squirrel breakfast with fried potatoes, gravy, and biscuits after an early morning hunt. Here's a hearty stew for later in the day. All the real lazy hunters like me just use chicken.

LYNCHBURG LAZY MAN'S SQUIRREL (CHICKEN) STEW

★★★★★★★★★★★★★★★★★★★★★★★★★★★★

8 boneless, skinless chicken thighs, cut into 2-inch chunks
   or 4 squirrels, cut up
Flour, salt and pepper
3 tablespoons bacon drippings or oil
1 large onion, chopped (about 1 1/2 cups)
4 ribs celery, sliced
1 bay leaf
2 cans (14 ounces each) chicken broth
1 can (28 ounces) diced tomatoes
2 cups frozen shoepeg corn
2 cups frozen baby lima beans
4 medium boiling potatoes, cut into 1-inch chunks
Hot pepper sauce, to taste

Chicken—Dredge the chicken in flour seasoned with salt and pepper. Heat bacon drippings in a large soup pot. Add meat and brown on all sides. Stir in onion and celery and cook until vegetables are tender, about 5 minutes. Add the bay leaf, broth, and additional water, if needed, to cover the meat. Simmer about 15 minutes, adding more water if necessary. Stir in the tomatoes, corn, limas, and potatoes. Cover and simmer 30 minutes or until all the vegetables are tender. Season with additional salt, pepper, and hot pepper sauce.

Squirrel—Dredge the squirrel pieces in flour seasoned with salt and pepper. Follow the directions above except simmer the meat about 45 minutes. Remove squirrel pieces with a slotted spoon. Remove the meat from the bones and return the meat to the pot. Continue as directed above.
Makes 6 to 8 servings.

VEGETABLES
& SIDES

Mary's every single day, but you'll also love it for Sunday brunch. One time, things got a little too spirited in the kitchen when three different cooks, unaware of what the others had done, each added some hometown product to the recipe. At dinner that day, a gentleman guest took one bite and said, "Honey, these apples gonna need a chaser!"

Around here, we have a spring crop of small tart green apples perfect for frying. Otherwise, good crisp Granny Smith and Golden Delicious apples are ideal. We make this really sweet, but add sugar to your liking.

Miss Mary Bobo's Boarding House

MOST OFTEN REQUESTED RECIPES

LYNCHBURG CANDIED APPLES

★★★★★★★★★★★★★★★★★★★★★★★★★

3 tablespoons butter
6 cups peeled and sliced green apples
1/4 to 1/2 cup sugar
1/3 cup Jack Daniel's Tennessee Whiskey

Melt butter in a large skillet over medium heat. Cook apples in butter until just tender, about 5 minutes. Stir in sugar and Jack Daniel's. Continue to cook until juice has thickened, about 5 minutes. Serve warm. **Makes 6 servings.**

I f I had to choose among our many popular recipes, I'd say these dishes get the most attention.

Miss Mary's Chicken with Pastry
Boarding House Fried Chicken
Crispy Fried Catfish
Superlative Fried Okra

Lynchburg Candied Apples
Miss Mary's Fudge Pie
Everyday Sweet Red Pepper Relish
Sour Mash Sweet Potatoes

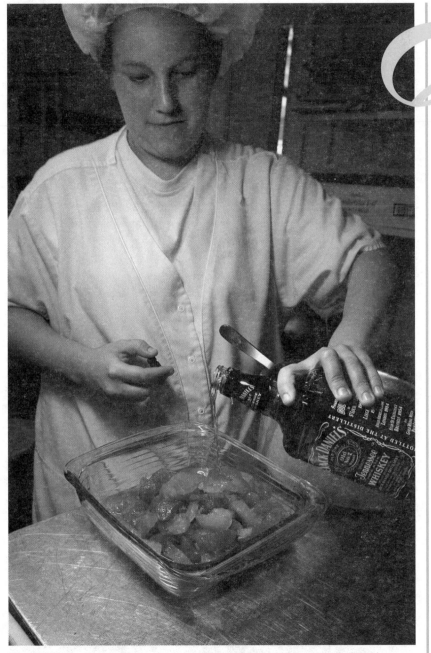

Jill carefully measures the secret ingredient in our Lynchburg Candied Apples.

A Nashville man said that he had been on the Internet that morning chatting with a fellow from Copenhagen, but had to sign off because he was headed to Lynchburg for a tour of the Jack Daniel Distillery. The man in Copenhagen asked, "Will you be eating at Miss Mary Bobo's?" He answered back, "Yes, how do you know about Miss Mary's?" The man replied that he'd eaten here and said, "Hope they're serving Lynchburg Candied Apples!"

Apples, fried okra is on the table every single day at Miss Mary's. Our secret is to let the okra sit in the cornmeal at least 30 minutes to dry. This important step keeps the coating from falling off during frying. Many of our guests from other countries and outside the South have never even seen okra, let alone tried it. One gentleman guest told me that the only time he'd ever seen okra was in canned vegetable soup where there would be one little slice floating around. He'd always throw it away! When entertaining friends at home, I serve fried okra in little baskets for a hot tidbit with cocktails. It's a fun conversation starter and sure beats plain old pretzels or peanuts.

SUPERLATIVE FRIED OKRA

★★★★★★★★★★★★★★★★★★★★★★★★

2 boxes (10 ounces) frozen sliced okra or 3 cups sliced fresh okra
2 cups self-rising cornmeal mix
Vegetable oil for frying
Salt, to taste

Let the frozen okra thaw and drain in a colander. Gently roll the okra a few at a time in cornmeal and coat each piece evenly. Set aside about 30 minutes to 1 hour to dry. Heat 1/2 to 1 inch of oil in a large skillet until hot (about 365°F). Add batches of okra in a single layer. Cook and roll gently with a fork or slotted spoon until browned on all sides. Remove with a slotted spoon and drain on paper towels. Season with salt and serve immediately. **Makes 8 servings.**

Pork fat and cured pork products have been flavoring Southern foods for generations. Once it was all we had, now we know it just tastes good. In addition to keeping bacon drippings in a jar in the refrigerator, here are other kinds of cured pork cuts we often use.

- **Hog Jowl**—The cheek meat of the hog that's most often smoked, cured, and sliced thicker than bacon. There's plenty of fat and flavor. Mother prefers it over bacon for flavoring beans and vegetables and even fries it for breakfast.

- **Sidemeat**—Similar to hog jowl, sidemeat comes from the flank of the pig. It's smoked, cured, sliced, and sold as bacon. Packages labeled "sidemeat" are fattier thick-sliced bacon used for seasoning.

- **Fat Back/Salt Pork**—Fatback, also known as salt pork, comes from the side and belly fat of the pig. It's salt-cured, but not smoked. Like all of them, we use it to season soups, beans, and vegetables.

- **Ham Hocks**—These are the ankle joints of the pig. They're available fresh, smoked, or cured. Add them to any slow-cooked dish like greens, beans, and soups.

- **Cracklings**—These are bits of fried pork skin. Around here they're sold already fried in small packages ready to add to cornbread batter for cracklin' cornbread.

- **City Ham/Country Ham**—Country ham is salted and dry-cured for months and is typical of the South. It has a salty rich meaty flavor and a dry texture. City ham is the everyday grocery store wet-cured variety. It's moist and less flavorful than country ham. Country ham is the best style for flavoring foods like pots of beans or greens.

- **Hambones**—A good country hambone is ideal for flavoring soups, beans, and greens. With all the country ham we serve in December, you can imagine the hambones we have stockpiled in our freezers. Just one of the many perks of the job! If you don't have a hambone handy, buy a little package of country ham scraps at the supermarket.

wild in the field behind Mother's house. In early spring, folks come from as far away as Fayetteville to fill up their baskets. We grew up on bitter turnip and tangy mustard greens, but you can fix this dish with kale or collards just as well. Heartier than soft spinach, traditional Southern greens are cooked until tender in a rich pork broth called pot likker. A smoked ham hock usually flavors the broth, but these days I often find it easier to use diced pork side meat, country ham scraps, sliced bacon, or bacon drippings. Any cured pork will nicely flavor the greens, but stay clear of any sweet flavored bacon. If you use a ham hock, simmer it in water for about 30 minutes. Then, remove the meat from the bone and return the meat to the pot when adding the greens. At the table pass the pepper vinegar and don't forget a hot skillet of cornbread.

EASY COUNTRY GREENS

★★★★★★★★★★★★★★★★★★★★★★★★★★

4 strips of bacon, diced, or 1/3 cup diced salt pork or diced country ham
    or 3 tablespoons bacon drippings
4 cups water
1 pound turnip, mustard, kale, or collard greens, washed, tough stems
    removed and cut into 2-inch pieces
Pinch of dried red pepper flakes
Salt, to taste
3 hard-boiled eggs, sliced or quartered

If using bacon or salt pork, fry it in a large pot until crisp. Add water to the pot and bring to a boil. If using country ham or bacon drippings, add to the hot water. Stir in the greens and dried red pepper flakes. Cover and simmer over low heat for 20 to 30 minutes or until greens are tender. Season with salt. Garnish serving bowl with eggs. Serve with pepper sauce or vinegar. **Makes 6 servings.**

Dee and I laughing with Mother over another one of her funny stories. Folks come to pick wild turnip greens in that hayfield behind us.

HEARD AROUND THE TABLE

During turnip green season one year a hostess told her table that she had been washing fresh greens in her washing machine. A Northern guest asked, "Doesn't it make a mess?" "No," she replied, "It was a bushel."

requested holiday dinner recipe. You'll find it on Miss Mary's tables at both seatings from December 1st through the 24th. By the time the New Year rolls around, the hostesses, cooks, and I are ready to retire this dish until the next December! Always boil the sweet potatoes with jackets on because the skin slides right off when cooked. It's up to your family tradition whether to top the sweet potatoes with toasted chopped pecans (I'm a pecan gal myself) or marshmallows. Why not both? Dee, of course, adds a little nutmeg!

COMMON
INGREDIENTS
giblet gravy

SOUR MASH SWEET POTATOES

★★★★★★★★★★★★★★★★★★★★★★★★★★★

4 large sweet potatoes
1/4 cup butter
3/4 cup brown sugar
1/8 teaspoon salt
1 tablespoon fresh orange zest
1/4 cup Jack Daniel's Tennessee Whiskey
1/2 cup lightly toasted chopped pecans

Place sweet potatoes in a large pot and cover completely with water. Add a little salt to the water. Bring to a boil, cover, and cook until tender, about 35 minutes. Drain and cool enough to handle. Peel off the skins and place the potatoes in a large mixing bowl. Mash the potatoes with the butter until slightly lumpy. Stir in sugar, salt, orange zest and Jack Daniel's. Spoon half the sweet potato mixture in a greased 2-quart baking dish. Sprinkle with half of the pecans. Repeat the layers. Bake at 350°F for about 30 minutes or until heated through. **Makes 8 servings.**

The rich giblet gravy we serve at Miss Mary's with holiday turkey and dressing often contains chopped hard-cooked eggs. It's a rural Tennessee tradition that dates back to when folks killed their own hens for dinner. The fresh hen would often contain an unlayed egg or two that we'd use to enrich the gravy. Quite a delicacy, the developing soft eggs are almost all yolk and have a mild buttery flavor.

TENNESSEE BUTTERNUT SQUASH

★★★★★★★★★★★★★★★★★★★★★★★★★★★★★

2 1/2 to 3 pounds (about 2 medium) butternut squash
Pinch of sugar
Salt and pepper, to taste
1 medium onion, chopped
2 cloves garlic, minced
3 tablespoons butter
1/4 cup Jack Daniel's Tennessee Whiskey
1 can (14 ounces) diced tomatoes, drained
1 1/2 cups sharp white Cheddar or Gruyere cheese

Heat the oven to 400°F. Grease a 9 x 13-inch baking dish. Split squash in half and scoop out seeds. Place halves cut side down in the baking dish. Cover lightly with foil and bake until tender, about 45 minutes. Remove from the oven and cool enough to handle. Scoop out the squash and place back in the greased baking dish. Season the squash with a pinch of sugar, salt and pepper; set aside.

Cook onion and garlic in butter in a medium skillet over medium heat until tender, about 5 minutes. Add Jack Daniel's and continue to cook until liquid has evaporated. Spoon the onion mixture over the squash. Top with tomatoes. Bake 20 minutes. Sprinkle with cheese and bake an additional 10 minutes or until cheese is melted and bubbly.
Makes 8 servings.

IF YOU MAY THINK THAT winter squash is impossible to fix without pools of butter and brown sugar, this recipe will change your mind. The creamy butternut squash combined with savory onions, acidic tomatoes, and earthy sharp cheddar cheese prove that opposites attract. It's a chic, colorful cold weather side dish that can be assembled ahead and baked just before serving. We love it with all kinds of poultry and pork. I've demonstrated this on television many times with great response from the TV crews.

delicious with pork, beef roast, or grilled steak. While it suits special occasions, when it's just Tom and me, I'll spoon it over split hot buttered biscuits for a creamy mushroom shortcake supper. It's a great first course, brunch dish, romantic supper, or sophisticated side. Season with salt and a little nutmeg at the end of cooking, keeping in mind the saltiness of your chicken broth. Miss Mary didn't care for nutmeg, but Dee sure does. Miss Mary scolded Dee many times about adding too much nutmeg to boarding house dishes. "When you die, Dee, I'm sprinkling a little nutmeg in your casket," Miss Mary would tease.

FANCY MUSHROOMS & PEARL ONIONS IN TENNESSEE CREAM SAUCE

★★★★★★★★★★★★★★★★★★★★★★★★★★

2 tablespoons butter
2 tablespoons olive oil
1 1/2 pounds assorted fresh mushrooms, quartered
1/3 cup Jack Daniel's' Tennessee Whiskey
2 cloves garlic, minced
8 ounces frozen pearl onions
1 cup heavy cream
1/2 cup chicken broth
Pinch of nutmeg, optional
Salt and pepper, to taste
Chopped fresh parsley

Heat butter and olive oil in a large skillet. Stir in mushrooms and cook over medium-high heat, stirring constantly until mushrooms appear dry, about 2 minutes. Stir in Jack Daniel's and garlic, bring to a boil, and simmer over medium-high heat until most of the liquid has evaporated, about 10 minutes. Mushrooms will shrink as they cook. Stir in the onions, cream, and chicken broth and bring to a boil. Simmer, stirring frequently, while the sauce reduces and thickens, about 10 minutes. Be patient and allow the sauce to thicken and nicely coat the vegetables. Season with nutmeg, salt and pepper. Sprinkle with parsley.
Makes 6 servings.

CREOLE RED AND GREEN BEANS

★★★★★★★★★★★★★★★★★★★★★★★★★★

1 pound green beans, trimmed and cut in half
   (or use frozen green beans)
2 stalks celery, finely chopped
1 medium green pepper, finely chopped
1 medium onion, finely chopped
2 cloves garlic, minced
3 tablespoons bacon drippings or butter
1 can (28 ounces) diced tomatoes
A pinch to 1/4 cup sugar, to taste
Salt and pepper, to taste

Cook green beans in boiling salted water in a large saucepan until tender. Drain, return to the pot, and set aside. Cook celery, green pepper, onion, and garlic in the drippings in a large skillet over medium heat until tender, about 5 minutes. Stir in the tomatoes and simmer, uncovered, about 10 to 15 minutes, or until thickened. Gently stir the tomato mixture into the green beans. Season with sugar, salt and pepper. Heat through. **Makes 8 servings.**

I'LL LET YOU IN ON A little secret to cooking vegetables the Southern way: a pinch of sugar. We add a pinch of sugar to just about everything at Miss Mary's, from pinto beans to turnip greens. Not enough to taste, but enough to balance the flavors. Mother has been making these green beans my whole life, usually with home-canned tomatoes and green beans. Now it's a boarding house classic during the holiday season. Of course, we tend to cook our green beans a little more thoroughly than much of the rest of the world. You can cook the beans until bright green and crisp tender, about 5 minutes, or like us for at least 20 minutes!

cornbread dressing is all anybody ever makes to go with the holiday roast turkey or a Sunday roast chicken. We don't call it "stuffing" as in other parts of the country, maybe because we typically cook it alongside the bird in a big casserole. Forget the store-bought "cornbread stuffing" crumbs. We always use the real thing. Keep leftover cornbread and biscuits in the freezer so a pan of dressing is never a chore. Our basic recipe contains the traditional celery, onions, and sage, and often good pork sausage. Soft inside and crispy on top, good dressing holds up nicely under gravy. Mother stirs in an egg or two with the broth for a lighter, puffier texture. Believe me, this is the dish most often passed around for seconds and thirds.

REAL CORNBREAD DRESSING

★★★★★★★★★★★★★★★★★★★★★★★★★★★

6 cups crumbled skillet cornbread
3 cups toasted bread or leftover biscuit cubes
1 cup chopped celery
1 cup chopped onion
1/4 cup plus 2 tablespoons butter
1 tablespoon dried sage
2 teaspoons black pepper
2 to 3 cups turkey or chicken broth

Heat oven to 350°F. Grease a 9 x 13-inch baking dish. Combine cornbread and bread cubes in a large mixing bowl. Cook celery and onion in 1/4 cup of the butter in a large skillet over medium heat until tender, about 5 minutes. Add cooked vegetables, sage, and pepper to cornbread. Stir in enough broth to moisten; blend well. Spoon it into the greased baking dish. Dot with the remaining 2 tablespoons of butter. Bake until golden brown and heated through, about 35 to 40 minutes. **Makes 10 to 12 servings.**

Experiment in the kitchen and create your own favorite cornbread dressing. Try adding any of the following to the basic recipe:

Chopped toasted pecans
Fresh chopped parsley
Chopped fresh apple
Raisins and other dried fruits
Bits of country ham
Cooked pork sausage
Any kind of cooked smoked sausage like kielbasa, andouille, or chorizo
Sautéed red and green bell peppers
Shredded cooked greens
Crisp crumbled bacon
Herbs like rosemary, thyme, marjoram, and oregano

SWEET TOMATO SUPPER PUDDING

★★★★★★★★★★★★★★★★★★★★★★★★★★★★

1 medium onion, chopped
1/2 cup (1 stick) butter
2 cans (28 ounces each) whole tomatoes with the juice
1/2 cup sugar
1 teaspoon dried basil
4 cups toasted white bread cubes
Black pepper, to taste
1 1/2 cups grated sharp white cheddar cheese
   or 3/4 cup grated Parmesan cheese, optional

Heat oven to 375°F. Grease a 9 x 13-inch baking dish. Cook onion in butter in a large saucepan over medium heat until softened, about 5 minutes. Stir in tomatoes and sugar. Cook and stir until the sugar has dissolved. Stir in basil, bread cubes, and pepper. Pour into the greased baking dish. Bake for 20 minutes. Sprinkle with cheese and bake an additional 10 minutes. **Makes 8 to 10 servings.**

Y ears ago, when everyone put up fruits and vegetables, Mother would occasionally visit the extension service cannery. She loved it because all you had to do was buy your jars, while they supplied free advice and equipment. Mother always wondered why the only folks she ever ran into down there were doctors' wives, not the rural families it was intended for. She always canned the best tomatoes and tomato juice. Her secret, of course, which she learned from her mother, was a pinch of sugar and salt in each jar. "Otherwise, they're not fit to eat, don't you think?"

NO, THAT'S NOT A TYPO, this really is a sweet TOMATO pudding meant to go with pork chops or just about any grilled meat and vegetable. Folks used to make sweet stewed tomato side dishes with stale bread and their home canned tomatoes during the winter and spring months. Miss Mary's traditional version doesn't call for onion or cheese, but I like this tasty modern update. These days, I might even sprinkle some chopped fresh basil on top.

here's another reason to stash some leftover cornbread in the freezer. At Miss Mary's we use cornbread crumbs on many of our vegetable casseroles because cornbread and vegetables are just a natural combination. And, I may sound like a broken record by now, but here is yet another dish that can benefit from the flavorful qualities of country ham bits. Feel free to substitute bacon drippings for the butter when cooking the vegetables. If you add country ham, be careful when adding additional salt. I know plenty of folks who would top this popular casserole with buttery cracker crumbs.

CHEDDAR SQUASH CASSEROLE WITH CRISPY CORNBREAD CRUMBS

★★★★★★★★★★★★★★★★★★★★★★★★★

1 large onion, chopped
1/4 cup plus 2 tablespoons butter
10 cups sliced yellow squash
1/2 cup water
Salt and pepper, to taste
2 cups grated cheddar cheese
1 jar (2 ounces) chopped pimientos, undrained
1/4 to 1/2 cup finely chopped country ham, optional
2 cups cornbread crumbs

Heat oven to 375°F. Grease a 9 x 13-inch baking dish. Cook onion in 1/4 cup of the butter in a large saucepan over medium heat until tender, stirring occasionally, about 5 minutes. Add squash and water. Reduce heat; cover and simmer about 20 minutes. Mash squash with a fork to break up large pieces. Stir in cheese and pimientos. Continue to cook a few more minutes, uncovered, until thick and creamy. Stir in country ham, if desired. Pour the squash into the greased baking dish. Sprinkle cornbread crumbs evenly over the top. Dot with the remaining 2 tablespoons of butter. Bake 20 minutes or until bubbly and the topping is golden brown. **Makes 8 servings.**

MASHED POTATOES AU GRATIN

★★★★★★★★★★★★★★★★★★★★★★★★★★★★★

4 pounds russet baking potatoes, peeled and cut into
   1 1/2-inch chunks
1 cup hot milk
1 cup sour cream
1/4 cup butter
Salt, to taste
3 eggs, beaten
2 cups grated sharp cheddar cheese

Heat oven to 400°F. Grease a 2-quart shallow baking dish. Cover potatoes with salted water in a large pot. Bring water to a boil and simmer potatoes until tender, about 20 minutes. Drain and return potatoes to the pot. Mash potatoes with milk, sour cream, and butter until smooth. Season with salt, to taste. Stir in eggs and 1 1/2 cups of the cheese. Spread the potatoes in the greased baking dish leaving the top bumpy. Sprinkle with remaining 1/2 cup of the cheese. Bake for 30 minutes or until heated through and the top begins to brown.
Makes 8 servings.

At Miss Mary's we tend to bake lots of our vegetable dishes and desserts in convenient 9 x 13-inch baking dishes and pans. It's just easier. Steaming pans of creamy squash, broccoli, or cabbage casserole, fruit cobblers, and sheet cakes became ingrained in our culture generations ago when much of small town socializing at church suppers, community meetings, and family gatherings called for bringing a dish to share. The 9 x 13-inch pan is still a kitchen necessity when cooking for a crowd or ensuring plenty of delicious leftovers.

I CALL THIS EASY CASSEROLE a blend of au gratin and mashed potatoes. Before serving, sprinkle the top with bits of country ham or crumbled bacon and fresh chives. The eggs lighten the texture of the potatoes while the top develops a golden crust. Sometimes I'll turn it into a main dish by adding cooked chopped onions and leftover sausage or chopped baked ham. Try it with other cheeses, a spoonful or two of prepared horseradish, or Dijon mustard.

CASSEROLE CULTURE

married a good country cook. Many a time he'd show up for midday dinner with unexpected guests just to show off Mother's cooking. She never knew how many places to set, but she did start to notice that certain salesmen and one particular preacher always paid a visit to Daddy's store just before noon. Today, her fried corn is still the specialty most often requested by her grandchildren. Fried corn is not really fried, but simply cooked in bacon drippings or butter until creamy and thickened. Mother says to do at least a dozen ears if you're going to the trouble. We prefer any white corn over yellow. We think it's sweeter, whether it is or not!

MOTHER'S BEST FRIED CORN

★★★★★★★★★★★★★★★★★★★★★★★

1/4 cup (1/2 stick) butter or bacon drippings
12 ears of sweet corn, kernels removed
1 cup water
Pinch or two of sugar
Salt, to taste

Melt butter in a large skillet over medium-high heat. Add corn, water, and sugar. Cook and stir about 20 minutes or until the corn mixture turns milky and thickens. If it seems too thin, add a tablespoon of cornstarch dissolved in 3 tablespoons of water and continue to cook until bubbly and thickened. **Makes 6 servings.**

When cutting corn off the cob, stand the cob on its end and cut half the kernels with a very sharp knife. Next, scrape down the cob with the back of the knife to extract the rest of the kernel and the juices without dulling the knife blade.

Mother, Daddy and Me. Reagor Motlow took this when I was about fourteen years old. We always had Christmas Dinner at the Motlows. Daddy's highest compliment to Mother was to tell her she looked better than a $500 mule. And she certainly did that day!

After reserving their seats just the day before, a couple from England visited us and they sat at my table. While I was out of the room, the gentleman told everyone at the table that when he called to see if we had room for them he got to laughing so hard that he could barely speak. He said that I sounded like something from out of *Gone with the Wind.* Said he never knew people actually talked like that—he thought it was just "movie talk."

experts, but macaroni and cheese is ever-present on dinner tables around here. In fact, at Miss Mary's we serve it all year—even during the holiday season. Everyone requests this recipe and everyone is surprised by our simple method. We use good old processed American cheese and the old Italian trick of adding some starchy pasta water to the sauce. Processed cheese makes a creamy, reliable sauce unlike aged cheddar that turns clumpy and rubbery when combined with water. Instead, sprinkle a little sharp cheddar on the top and a few bread crumbs, if you like.

BOARDING HOUSE BAKED MACARONI AND CHEESE

★★★★★★★★★★★★★★★★★★★★★★★★★

1 box (16 ounces) elbow macaroni
2 pounds processed American cheese
1 teaspoon dry mustard
Salt and pepper, to taste
1 cups grated sharp cheddar cheese
3/4 cup coarse bread crumbs, optional

Heat the oven to 375°F. Grease a 9 x 13-inch baking dish. Cook macaroni in salted water according to package directions. When the macaroni is cooked, but before straining, use a ladle to remove 3 cups of the macaroni water and set aside. Strain macaroni and return it to the pot. Add the reserved water and processed cheese to the pot. Stir the macaroni over low heat until the cheese melts. It will seem a bit watery, but the macaroni will absorb most of the liquid during baking. Pour the mixture into the greased pan. Bake for 20 minutes or until hot and bubbly. Top with the cheddar cheese and bread crumbs. Bake an additional 10 minutes, or until the cheese has melted.
Makes 8 to 10 servings.

PEPPER JACK RICE BAKE

★★★★★★★★★★★★★★★★★★★★★★★★★★

1 medium red bell pepper, chopped
1 medium onion, chopped
2 tablespoons oil
1 1/2 cups rice, cooked according to package directions (6 cups cooked)
8 ounces sour cream
1 can (10.75 ounces) condensed cream of celery soup
2 cans (4.5 ounces each) chopped green chilies
1 cup roasted corn kernels
2 cups grated pepper Jack or Monterey Jack cheese, divided
Salt and pepper, to taste

Heat oven to 375°F. Grease a 9 x 13-inch baking dish. Cook bell pepper and onion in oil in a large skillet over medium-high heat until softened, about 5 to 7 minutes. Combine cooked rice, sour cream, soup, green chilies, corn, and cooked peppers and onion and 1 cup of the cheese in a large mixing bowl. Blend well. Season with salt and pepper.

Pour into the greased baking dish. Cover with foil and bake 30 minutes. Remove cover and sprinkle with remaining 1 cup of cheese. Bake an additional 10 minutes or until cheese is melted and the casserole is bubbly. **Makes 8 to 10 servings.**

MOTHER TAUGHT US TO make the most of everything, including leftovers. Sort of like sour mash, a little of last night's supper usually shows up in the next day's meal. This rice casserole is just one of those happy accidents that occurred when I found myself with a few extra ears of roasted corn. This peppery variation of a popular Miss Mary's casserole includes roasted corn kernels and even some red bell pepper that you can roast or cook in a pan with onion. The pepper Jack cheese adds a nice kick. Use hot green chilies, too, if you like.

Miss Mary Bobo's Boarding House
HOLIDAY MENU

Six days a week during the month of December, we serve our special Tennessee holiday dinner. Trouble is, if you're looking to make reservations this year, you're probably out of luck. Most folks and dinner groups will sign up for next year as they walk out the door this year. But, you're never too late to get on a waiting list! Still, you can always enjoy a little of our Lynchburg holiday spirit in your own home, wherever you live, by simply preparing a few of our dishes. I'd recommend you not miss out on both the Sour Mash Sweet Potatoes and our Lynchburg Cranberry Relish.

Served December 1 through 24, six days a week:
Roast Turkey
Baked Country Ham
Cornbread Dressing
Giblet Gravy
Fried Okra
Lynchburg Cranberry Relish
Sour Mash Sweet Potatoes
Creole Red and Green Beans
Boarding House Baked Macaroni and Cheese
Southern Spoon Rolls
Pumpkin Patch Squares with Cream Cheese Icing

After preparing, serving and eating our holiday dinner six days a week for three weeks, my cooks, hostesses, and I are all ready for something different. When we get together for our own holiday affair, we all hop on over to Tullahoma, about ten miles down the road, for a night of fun, rest, and revelry at the pizza parlor! Isn't that just like people!

DINNER

Bedford is well known throughout Moore County for more than just his good tasting whiskey. Jimmy cures and smokes his own country hams in the smoke house on his farm. These days country hams are more readily available than ever. Here's Jimmy's quick ham glaze which I like because it complements the saltiness of a good country ham.

TENNESSEE
Country Ham

JIMMY BEDFORD'S COUNTRY HAM GLAZE

★★★★★★★★★★★★★★★★★★★★★★★★★

3/4 cup brown sugar
1/4 cup Jack Daniel's Tennessee Whiskey
1/2 cup coarse-grained mustard

Follow the manufacturer's directions for cooking your ham. Rub the cooked ham with the glaze after you've cut off the skin and fat. Bake at 400°F about 20 minutes or until the glaze caramelizes on the ham.

We serve country ham at room temperature very thinly sliced. An electric knife makes the neatest slices. We carve up such a storm at Miss Mary's that our electric knives just burn out from exhaustion several times a year.

HOW TO BAKE A TENNESSEE COUNTRY HAM IN A BAG OR ON A RACK IN A ROASTER

- **Scrub all mold off the ham.** Soak overnight in cold water.
- **Saw off the hock,** if you like.
- **Place ham (skin-side up so it will baste itself) in an oven cooking bag.** Pour in about 1 quart of water. Tie the bag tightly around the ham so that the water will rise up about halfway up the ham.*
- **Place in a shallow roasting pan** that the ham will comfortably fit in-- not too big or too small.
- **Roast 20 minutes per pound** at 325°F. The internal temperature should be 160°F when the ham is done and the bone will feel loose. Jerk out the bone and save it for a pot of beans.
- **Cool slightly.** Cut skin and fat off the ham, if desired. Coat with Jimmy Bedford's Country Ham Glaze and bake at 400°F about 20 minutes or until the glaze caramelizes on the ham. Wrap securely in foil. Store in the refrigerator.
  *Or, place the trimmed ham fat-side up on a rack in a roasting pan with 2 inches of water. Cover tightly with foil. Bake as directed above.

CRISPY FRIED CATFISH OR CRAPPIE

★★★★★★★★★★★★★★★★★★★★★★★★★★★★★★★★

Vegetable oil for frying
1 cup white cornmeal or self-rising cornmeal mix
1/4 cup flour
2 eggs
1/2 cup milk
6 to 10 catfish fillets or about 3 pounds crappie fillets
Salt and pepper, to taste

Heat about 1 to 2 inches oil in a heavy iron skillet to 365°F. Combine cornmeal and flour in a shallow bowl. In a separate bowl, beat eggs and milk and blend well. Season the fish with salt and pepper. Dip fish in the egg mixture and then dip in the cornmeal mixture, coating all sides. Shake off excess. Let coated fillets rest a few minutes before cooking.

Fry a few pieces of fish at a time in the hot oil until golden brown on all sides. Cooking time depends on the thickness of the fish. Test for doneness by piercing with a fork or the tip of a knife in the thickest part of the fish. The fish is cooked through if the flesh is opaque and flakes easily. Drain on paper towels. Serve with hushpuppies and Jack's Red Dipping Sauce (see page 27). **Makes 6 servings.**

Incredible as it may sound, country ham is a major topic of discussion at the annual Tennessee Walking Horse National Celebration held down the road in Shelbyville the week before Labor Day. The horses are magnificent, but it's the country ham sandwiches (sliced salty ham always served on soft hamburger buns) sold by a variety of vendors that sustain the crowd of thousands through long days of events. My family and plenty of our friends have held box seats for the celebration as long as I can remember. And every year it doesn't take long for word to get around who's making the best sandwiches. We feel obliged to try them all.

George Gregory keeps things beautiful around here planting trees, cutting grass and tending to the rose garden around the town square gazebo. Otherwise, you'll find him crappie fishing on Tims Ford Lake. Every spring Lynchburg's expert angler empties out the freezer and holds a fish fry for all the Distillery families. That's pretty much all of us. It's true, we don't bother with fish too much if it isn't fried. There's just something about the steaming white, moist flaky meat wrapped in a delicate crisp crust. Many folks don't bother with the egg wash like in this recipe. Dee simply dredges the fillets in the cornmeal and fries it up in a skillet. Her other secret is to give frozen fish a saltwater soak before frying and you'd never know it came from the freezer.

SOME FOLKS PREFER
panfrying boneless, skinless chicken breasts instead of frying the whole bird. I'll admit that it's a lot easier. Dress them up with a savory sauce featuring a little Jack and mustard or add a spoonful of orange marmalade for exotic sweetness. You'll also have good luck using the more flavorful boneless, skinless chicken thighs in this recipe.

PANFRIED TENNESSEE WHISKEY CHICKEN BREASTS

★★★★★★★★★★★★★★★★★★★★★★★★★

6 boneless, skinless chicken breast halves
Salt and pepper
1/2 cup all-purpose flour
2 plus 3 tablespoons butter
2 tablespoons oil
2 tablespoons minced onion
1 cup chicken broth
1/4 cup Jack Daniel's Tennessee Whiskey
1 tablespoon coarse-grained Dijon mustard

Sprinkle the chicken with salt and pepper. Place the flour in a shallow bowl. Coat the chicken pieces evenly with flour, shaking off the excess. Heat 2 tablespoons of the butter and the oil in a large cast-iron or nonstick skillet until hot. Place half the chicken pieces in the skillet. Cook 4 to 5 minutes without turning. Flip the chicken over and cook 4 to 5 minutes. Remove to a platter and keep the chicken warm.

Cook the remaining chicken. Add onion to the drippings in the skillet. Cook over medium heat until soft, about 3 minutes. Stir in the broth and Jack Daniel's. Increase heat to high and boil the liquid until thickened, stirring frequently, about 5 minutes. Stir in the mustard and remaining butter. Pour the sauce over the chicken. Serve immediately.

Makes 6 servings.

The six Master Distillers of the Jack Daniel Distillery. That's Uncle Jack top left followed clockwise by Jimmy Bedford, Frank Bobo, Jess Gamble, my Uncle Lem Tolley and my Great-Uncle Jess Motlow.

HEARD AROUND THE TABLE

Our hostess Lila told her table of Yankee guests that in the South we split the biscuit and put chicken gravy over it. The man on her right picked up his biscuit, split it, and while holding it in his hand, dabbed it with a quarter-sized spot of gravy on the bottom, replaced the top, and set it on his plate.

MEET
Jimmy Bedford

As the sixth Master Distiller for the Jack Daniel Distillery, my friend and neighbor Jimmy Bedford is the man responsible for making my Uncle Jack's Tennessee Whiskey consistently excellent year after year. It's a big responsibility and we have nothing to worry about with Jimmy's mellow approach.

When you come to visit us in Lynchburg, you'll probably see Jimmy's beautiful farm on the right about two miles from town coming from Tullahoma. When he's not smoking his country hams, running the tractor or busy at the Distillery, there's a chance you could run into him anywhere in the world, talking to folks about our fine hometown product.

Since Uncle Jack passed on in 1911, only four other men besides Jimmy have held the title "Master Distiller." They were my grandmother's brother Jess Motlow (1911–1941), my Uncle Lem Tolley (1941-1964), Jess Gamble (1964-1966) and Frank Bobo (1966-1992).

steaks, but there's nothing like the crust you can only get from panfrying meat in a hot, hot iron skillet. You must have plenty of ventilation in the kitchen for this method. To keep the smoke outside, use your outdoor gas grill side burner or turkey fryer burner. This is about as man-pleasing a recipe as I know. Get to know your butcher and have those steaks cut nice and thick.

SKILLET STEAKS WITH LYNCHBURG PAN SAUCE

★★★★★★★★★★★★★★★★★★★★★★★★★★

2 porterhouse or T-bone steaks, about 1 1/2 to 2 inches thick
Vegetable oil
Salt and pepper
2 tablespoons butter
1 tablespoon Worcestershire sauce
1/4 cup Jack Daniel's Tennessee Whiskey

Heat a large cast-iron skillet over high heat until very hot, about 10 minutes. Generously rub steaks with oil and sprinkle with salt and pepper. Cook steaks one at time. Sear steak on one side, about 5 minutes. Flip and cook an additional 5 minutes for medium-rare; 6 minutes for medium. Remove the steak from the skillet and keep warm. Repeat with the second steak and keep warm.

Melt the butter in the skillet; stir in the Worcestershire sauce and Jack Daniel's. Bring to a boil and cook about 2 minutes. Slice steaks, if desired. Pour sauce over steaks and serve immediately.
Makes 4 servings.

TOLLEY TOWN BEEF STEW

★★★★★★★★★★★★★★★★★★★★★★★★★★★★★

4 pounds beef chuck roast, cut into 2-inch chunks
1/2 cup all-purpose flour
About 1/4 cup bacon drippings or oil
3 medium onions, chopped
2 ribs celery, chopped
2 large carrots, chopped
4 cloves garlic, minced
1 can (14.5 ounces) diced tomatoes, undrained
1 cup Jack Daniel's Tennessee Whiskey
2 cups beef broth
2 tablespoons Dijon mustard
2 bay leaves
1 package (16 ounces) mushrooms, halved or quartered
1 package (16 ounces) frozen pearl onions
Salt and pepper, to taste
Chopped fresh parsley

Heat the oven to 350°F. Toss meat with flour in a large bowl. Heat 2 tablespoons of the bacon drippings in a large Dutch oven with an oven-proof lid. Brown meat on all sides over medium-high heat in 3 batches. Add more drippings as necessary. Set meat aside. Add onion, celery, and carrots. Cook over medium heat until the onions are tender and just begin to brown, about 8 minutes. Stir in the garlic and continue to cook an additional 2 minutes. Stir in the meat, tomatoes, Jack Daniel's, beef broth, mustard, and bay leaves. Bring to a boil. Cover and cook in the oven for 2 hours. Stir in the mushrooms and pearl onions. Season with salt and pepper. Cover and return to the oven and cook 1 hour or until the meat and vegetables are fork tender. Serve with egg noodles, grits, or potatoes. Sprinkle with parsley. **Makes 10 servings.**

THIS IS MY DOWN-HOME version of France's famous Boeuf Bourguignon and it's been a reliable standard for stress-free entertaining at my home. It seems to please everyone every time and allows me to experiment with different side dishes beyond my favorite green beans, peppery watercress salad, and buttery mashed potatoes.

SHRIMP AND SCALLOPS Á LA DANIEL

★★★★★★★★★★★★★★★★★★★★★★★★★★

2 tablespoons butter

2 tablespoons olive oil

12 jumbo shrimp, peeled and deveined

8 scallops, cut in half if very large

1 small onion, finely chopped

1/2 cup chopped red bell pepper

1/3 cup Jack Daniel's Tennessee Whiskey

1 cup heavy cream

Salt and pepper, to taste

1/2 pound fresh thin asparagus, cut into 1-inch pieces and cooked until
   just crisp-tender

1 pound cooked pasta

Chopped fresh parsley

Lemon wedges

Heat the butter and olive oil in a large skillet over medium-high heat. Add shrimp and scallops and cook until they just turn opaque, stirring frequently, about 3 to 4 minutes. Remove shrimp and scallops from the skillet. Set aside and keep warm. Cook onion and bell pepper in the drippings in the skillet over medium heat until softened, about 2 minutes. Remove the pan from the heat. Pour Jack Daniel's into a corner of the skillet; heat and carefully ignite, shaking the pan until the flames subside. Add cream, simmer until thickened and reduced by about 1/3. Season with salt and pepper. Stir in shrimp, scallops and asparagus and heat through. Serve over pasta. Sprinkle each serving with parsley and garnish with a lemon wedge. **Makes 6 servings.**

up the room and impress your guests with a showy flambé display. Actually, this creamy seafood dish is delicious with or without the fireworks. Serve it in big bowls over pasta like fettuccini or wide egg noodles and hunks of crusty bread to sop up the rich sauce. Don't forget a crisp green salad with vinaigrette.

Being an official Jack Daniel's taste-tester requires extraordinary focus and dedication. As you can imagine, there's always plenty of work to be done!

As a descendant of Jack Daniel and fourth generation Lynchburg native, I know it's in my blood to carry on the family tradition. Every single Friday, I join twenty-three other Distillery employees for the weekly taste-testing of the newest aged batches of Jack Daniel's. We compare the smell and taste of the current batch of Jack Daniel's whiskey to batches from the previous year. Our job is to find continuity from year to year so that every new bottle we sell tastes just as good as the last. We don't get paid extra for this work, but we do receive the coveted official duck decoy plaque after one year of service. No, I don't plan on quitting any time soon.

OFFICIAL
Taste-Testers

Invitational Barbecue Champion-ship Cook-Off contestants who compete in Lynchburg every Oc-tober may consider oven-cooked brisket to be a travesty. Not me. A brisket needs steady warm, moist heat so why not take advantage of the oven? After baking, you can grill the brisket for a little while to add a smoky char. But actually, I usually cook the brisket in the oven with a dash of liquid smoke slipped into the marinade. Be sure to get a flat brisket with a nice layer of fat to help tenderize the meat as it cooks.

KITCHEN BEEF BRISKET

1 (4 to 6 pounds) beef brisket
1 medium onion, finely chopped
1/4 cup Jack Daniel's Tennessee Whiskey
1/4 cup soy sauce
1/4 cup ketchup
1/4 cup brown sugar
1/4 cup cider vinegar
2 tablespoons Dijon mustard
1 tablespoon Worcestershire sauce
2 cloves garlic, minced
1/2 teaspoon liquid smoke, optional
Black pepper, to taste

Heat the oven to 300°F. Put brisket fat-side up in a roasting pan and sprinkle with the onion. Combine all the remaining ingredients in a large measuring cup. Pour over the brisket. Cover tightly with heavy duty aluminum foil. Bake about 4 hours or until the internal temperature reaches 190°F and meat is tender. Let the meat rest at least 10 minutes before carving across the grain into thin slices with a sharp knife. Serve with pan drippings.

Even better, cook the brisket a day before serving. Remove the cooked brisket from the drippings. Cover tightly with foil and refrigerate overnight. Refrigerate the drippings and skim off the hardened fat the next day. Before serving, slice the brisket while it's cold for a much neater cut. Combine the meat with the pan drippings in a baking dish. Cover and reheat at 325°F for about 30 minutes or until thoroughly warm. **Makes 10 servings.**

OVEN BBQ TENNESSEE PORK TENDERLOIN

★★★★★★★★★★★★★★★★★★★★★★★★★★

1/4 cup Jack Daniel's Tennessee Whiskey
1/4 cup soy sauce
1/4 cup ketchup
1/2 cup brown sugar
1/2 teaspoon garlic powder
2 pounds pork tenderloin

Heat the oven to 450°F. Combine all ingredients except the pork tenderloin in a small saucepan. Bring to a boil and simmer until slightly thickened, about 5 minutes. Place the tenderloin on a foil-lined baking or roasting pan. Brush with the sauce. Roast for about 30 minutes until the internal temperature is 150°F. Remove from the oven and let the meat rest about 10 minutes before slicing. **Makes 6 servings.**

I've found that a little cutting back is a good thing after traveling and indulging in rich meals. I've come up with a little diet of my own to keep me on track—and the key is chicken broth. We poach lots of chickens for Miss Mary's Chicken with Pastry so I always have plenty of it in the freezer. Mother and I enjoy rich broth with cooked rice for a light but filling supper.

WHEN OUTDOOR GRILLING is just out of the question, barbecued oven-roasted pork tenderloin is a clever alternative. This basting sauce is terrific on oven baked (or grilled) ribs as well. The sauce is very sticky so remember to line a baking or roasting pan with foil for easy clean-up. Serve the sliced pork with corncakes or Cast-Iron Cornbread (see page 48), white beans, and either the creamy White Mayo or Clear Vinegar Slaw (see pages 65). Now that's not a bad indoor picnic—even without the hickory smoke.

THE TOLLEY
Chicken Broth Diet

all-time favorites at Miss Mary's. You'll see that the creamy chicken mixture is pretty standard. What makes this dish so special is the delicious pastry made with lard. Our recipes may continue to evolve, but one thing we'll never give up is our loyalty to this historic tradition. Lard gives foods a savory richness that shortening lacks. We've shocked plenty of guests with the mention of the "L" word. I like to remind everyone that Miss Mary lived to be 102, and many of the old boarding house regulars lived well into their nineties. We like to attribute that to good wholesome eating—including lard. I certainly plan on following in their footsteps.

Don't throw out your pastry scraps. Cut them into pieces and place them on a cookie sheet. Brush with egg wash and sprinkle with cinnamon and sugar. Bake them in the oven with the casserole until golden brown. Treat yourself with sweet pastry strips right out of the oven.

MISS MARY'S CHICKEN WITH PASTRY OR BISCUIT DUMPLINGS

★★★★★★★★★★★★★★★★★★★★★★★★★★★★

CHICKEN
1 (2 1/2 to 3 pounds) chicken
1 large onion
1 rib celery
1 teaspoon salt
1/4 cup all-purpose flour
1/4 cup water
Salt and pepper, to taste

PASTRY
2 cups all-purpose flour
1 teaspoon salt
2/3 to 3/4 cup lard (more lard makes a more tender crust)
1/4 cup ice cold water

Place chicken, onion, celery, and salt in a large pot. Add enough water to completely cover the chicken. Bring to a boil; reduce heat and simmer until the chicken is tender and cooked through, about 1 hour. While chicken cooks, make the pastry. Remove the chicken from the broth so chicken can cool enough to handle. Pick chicken off the bones, discarding bones and skin. Spread chicken in a greased 9 x 13-inch baking dish and set aside.

Remove celery and onion from broth. Measure broth and return 3 cups to the pot. Combine the 1/4 cup flour with 1/4 cup water in a small bowl. Blend to make a smooth paste. Stir into the hot broth. Cook 5 to 10 minutes or until the broth is thickened. Season with salt and pepper. Pour over the chicken. Top with strips of pastry and bake at 400°F about 30 minutes or until the pastry is golden brown.

CONTINUED ON NEXT PAGE

To make the pastry: Combine flour and salt in a medium mixing bowl. Cut in shortening with a pastry blender or two knives until mixture forms coarse crumbs. Sprinkle with cold water and mix until dough holds together and will form a ball. Roll out on a floured board or pastry cloth to about 1/4 inch thickness. Cut into 2 x 13-inch strips.

Biscuit Dumpling: If making pastry isn't for you, make easy drop biscuit dumplings. Follow the recipe for Homemade Biscuits (see page 46), but use 1 cup of milk. Drop the soft dough by spoonfuls over the warm chicken mixture and bake at 400°F for 20 to 25 minutes or until golden brown. **Makes 6 to 8 servings.**

PLEASE PASS THE PORK ROAST

1 (about 5 pounds) pork loin roast
2 tablespoons Dry County Dry Rub (see page 125)
1 teaspoon onion powder
Zest from 1 lemon
3 green bell peppers, coarsely chopped
4 medium onions, sliced
1/3 cup flour
Salt and pepper, to taste

Heat the oven to 450°F. Combine the dry rub with onion powder and lemon zest in a small bowl. Rub the mixture onto all sides of the roast. Place the roast, fat-side up, on a rack in a roasting pan. Cook for 30 minutes or until well-browned. Remove the roast from the oven. Reduce the oven temperature to 350°F. Arrange the green peppers and onions around the roast. Add about 1 inch of hot water to the pan. Cover tightly with foil and return the roast to the oven and bake about 1 1/2 to 2 hours or until tender

CONTINUED ON NEXT PAGE

TRADITIONAL BOARDING house food is not about "one-dish" dinners of meats swimming together with vegetables in the same casserole. Our tables are crowded with platters of meats and gravy, bowls and casseroles of vegetable sides, and often a relish or two. The boarding house rule is to help yourself to the dish in front of you and pass to the left. By the time folks are starting on seconds, they're calling out for or offering a dish to the other end of the table. Our pork roast is popular for seconds and thirds along with mashed potatoes and our tangy Crispy Kraut Salad (see page 78). Any size roast will do, just alter the seasonings and vegetable amounts.

with an internal temperature of 175°F on a meat thermometer. Remove the roast from the pan and let rest on a board before slicing.

Pour the drippings and vegetables (about 8 cups) into a large saucepan and simmer. Combine the flour and 1/3 cup of water in a small bowl to make a paste. Add to the pan drippings, stirring constantly, until the gravy is bubbly and thickened, about 5 minutes. Season with salt and pepper. Slice the roast and serve it on a platter covered with the gravy and vegetables. **Makes about 8 servings.**

PANTRY SALMON CROQUETTES WITH CREOLE MUSTARD SAUCE

2 cans (14.75 ounces each) salmon, drained
1/2 cup grated onion
1 cup finely chopped celery
Juice of half a lemon (about 2 tablespoons)
1 tablespoon Worcestershire sauce
2 eggs, beaten
3/4 cup milk
1 1/2 cups cracker crumbs plus another 1 1/2 cups for breading the croquettes (about 2 sleeves of saltines)
Vegetable oil for frying
Creole Mustard Sauce (recipe follows)

Place salmon in a large bowl, removing skin and large bones. Flake with a fork. Stir in remaining ingredients except oil, using 1 1/2 cups of cracker crumbs. Blend well. Shape into croquettes using 1/3 cup of the

CONTINUED ON NEXT PAGE

WE'VE REVIVED THIS old favorite only recently at Miss Mary's. Keeping canned salmon in the pantry is most of the work, that and crushing a few crackers. Unlike most fried foods, you don't have to enjoy the croquettes right away. They'll keep crisp and hot in a warm oven until serving time. Make the Creole Mustard Sauce as tangy as you like and pass the sauce at the table (always to the left, of course). Use 1 can of salmon and cut the recipe in half for about 6 croquettes, but you'll miss the leftovers.

mixture for each. Gently coat with remaining cracker crumbs and let rest on a cookie sheet. Heat 1/2 inch of oil in a large skillet over medium-high heat. Fry a few croquettes at a time until golden brown and crisp, about 3 to 4 minutes per side. Keep cooked croquettes in a warm oven while frying the rest. Serve with Creole Mustard Sauce.

Makes 6 to 8 servings, about 13 croquettes.

CREOLE MUSTARD SAUCE

5 tablespoons butter
5 tablespoons all-purpose flour
1 cup chicken broth
1 cup milk
2 tablespoons Creole mustard or other coarse-grained mustard, to taste
1 cup frozen green peas
Salt and pepper, to taste

Melt butter in a small saucepan over medium heat. Stir in flour and cook until smooth and bubbly, about 1 minute. Gradually stir in broth and milk. Bring to a boil and simmer until thickened. Stir in mustard and peas. Season with salt and pepper. Cook until peas are heated through.

Makes about 3 cups.

HEARD AROUND THE TABLE

A couple visiting from Australia shared their woeful tale about a traffic ticket they received near Chattanooga for driving on the wrong side of the road. Sympathetic to this news, their dinner companions all chipped in to settle their fine.

everytime I hear what fancy chefs nowadays call "free range" chicken. Every spring Daddy used to buy a cage full of baby chicks down at the general store and raise them in the chicken yard out back until they weighed about two pounds. Mother simply cut the tender little dressed birds in half, dusted them with seasoned flour and tossed them in a skillet of hot lard. Our master distiller Jimmy Bedford grew up watching his mother Wilma snag a little fryer, pecking and scratching out in the yard, and have it fried and on the table for breakfast. Of course, breakfast wasn't complete without a plateful of hot homemade biscuits and gravy made from the pan drippings. Dip the chicken in egg before flouring for a thicker crust. Here's to the original "free range" chicken fried in lard that we still serve at Miss Mary's today.

MOTHER'S FRIED CHICKEN

★★★★★★★★★★★★★★★★★★★★★★★

1 (1 1/2 to 3 pounds) chicken (the smaller the better)
Salt, to taste
2 eggs, beaten
1/4 cup milk or buttermilk
2 cups flour, seasoned with salt and pepper
3 cups lard

Cut chicken into pieces. Rinse and pat dry. Season chicken with salt. Beat eggs in a shallow bowl with the milk. Place seasoned flour in another shallow bowl. Dip chicken pieces into egg wash and then in seasoned flour, coating well. Set aside to dry for about 15 minutes. Heat lard in large iron skillet. When the fat is hot (365°F), carefully place the chicken pieces in the skillet, but don't overcrowd the skillet. Cook until the chicken is golden brown on one side. Turn and brown the other side. Reduce the heat to medium-low. Cover the pan and cook for 10 minutes per side. Uncover, increase heat, and cook about 5 minutes to crisp chicken. Chicken is done when the meat juices run clear when pierced with the tip of a knife. The smaller the pieces, the less time it will take to cook.
Makes 4 servings.

THREE SECRETS TO FRIED CHICKEN SUCCESS: SMALL BIRDS, CAST IRON, AND LARD

- **Small Birds**—These days grocery store birds tend to be on the large side. Avoid the big roasters and use the smallest bird labeled "fryer" you can find and cut it up yourself. The smaller breast pieces cook evenly, don't dry out as quickly, and have a good ratio of crispy skin to juicy meat. If you use large breasts, cut them in half.
- **Cast Iron**—Even heating is essential for good frying. Heavy cast iron is the best choice because it heats more evenly and retains heat better than other metals. The added bonus of frying is that it's a great way to keep your iron skillet seasoned for making cornbread.
- **Lard**—Lard gives chicken the proper slightly earthy flavor and crisp texture necessary for real Southern fried chicken. There's just nothing like it.

STEPS FOR PERFECT FRIED CHICKEN

- **Pick small whole birds** that weigh no more than 3 1/2 pounds at the grocery store (not the big roasting birds) and cut them up yourself.
- **Cut 11 pieces,** including a pully bone. Cut off the wings, legs, and thighs. Cut around the pully bone (wishbone) so you have a long skinny piece with 2 meaty ends of breast meat. Cut the breast in half and cut 2 side breasts (more like backs).
- **Rinse and dry the pieces,** season with salt, dip in beaten egg, if you like (some folks dip in egg, buttermilk, sweet milk, or sometimes nothing) and simply coat the piece in seasoned flour. Let the pieces dry for about 15 minutes so the coating adheres to the chicken during frying.
- **Use an iron skillet.** Fry the pieces in batches in about 1 inch of hot lard (365°F on a deep-fry thermometer) without crowding the skillet.
- **Brown the pieces over high heat** on both sides. Reduce the heat and cover the skillet to get the meat cooked through and the juices to run clear. Five minutes before it's done, remove the lid. Increase the heat and crisp both sides. Practice makes perfect.

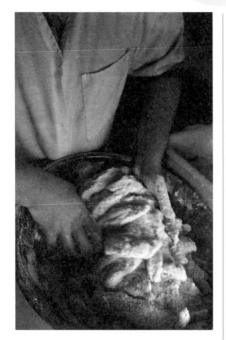

My cousin Chris holds the catfish fillets between his fingers to keep them separate before gently dropping them into the hot oil.

THE BUSINESS
of Frying

Many folks' exposure to fried foods is limited to restaurants. With a little care and attention, home frying is easy and fun now and again. The goal is to use enough hot oil to quickly crisp the outside and cook the food throughout. Use plenty of oil to cover the food completely. Be sure the oil is hot, about 365°F on a deep-fry thermometer. If the oil is too hot, the food will burn on the outside and remain raw on the inside.

If the oil is not hot enough, the fried food will be greasy, tough, and bland.

Always fry foods in small batches in evenly cut pieces that have been thoroughly thawed and patted dry. Lower the pieces gently into the oil. Have a bowl or platter lined with paper towels ready for the hot cooked food. Let the hot oil fully cool before discarding.

SUPPER OUTSIDE

down the road in Fayetteville, Tennessee, where her daddy had a commercial barbecue pit during his "retirement" years. This was my Granddaddy's special sauce and I've never seen another like it. Pickle juice is the main acid and thinly sliced lemons, rind and all, cook down in the sauce. My cousin Jim Dickey, also a fine pitmaster, uses it all the time as a mop sauce for pork. He omits the sugar and Worcestershire sauce so the sugars won't burn while cooking.

Empty Barrels Have Many Uses

DAD'S BARBECUE SAUCE

★★★★★★★★★★★★★★★★★★★★★★★★★

1 medium onion, grated
1/2 cup (1 stick) butter
1 cup dill pickle juice
1/4 cup cider vinegar
1/2 cup sugar
2 lemons, thinly sliced
2 teaspoons crushed red pepper
2 teaspoons cayenne pepper
2 tablespoons Worcestershire sauce
Salt and black pepper, to taste

Cook onion in butter in a small saucepan over medium heat until softened, about 5 minutes. Stir in the remaining ingredients and simmer about 20 minutes. Use as a barbecue baste or serve warm on the side. Keep unused portion refrigerated. **Makes about 2 cups.**

You may be wondering what we do with all those used oak barrels. The federal regulation says we can age our whiskey in them only one time. Because our used barrels are still full of flavor, many go to our whiskey distillery friends in Scotland. In fact, you may have one sitting on your patio full of petunias. Half a barrel makes a handy planter and grows happy plants. We also bust up a few to make our popular Jack Daniel's smoking chips and flavor pellets for outdoor grilling and barbecuing.

Here's the view from our front porch. We live just two miles from the town square so I can never blame traffic for being late to work.

HEARD AROUND THE TABLE

A lady from Texas said that her husband liked Jack Daniel's so much that he kept some in a spray bottle in the refrigerator to spray on food. I asked her what he sprayed it on. She said "ice cream, brownies, pecan pie, and barbecue."

Lynchburg-style barbecue sauce—tangy with a good bit of vinegar, sweet and spicy, but not as ketchupy and sweet as the sauces to our west in Memphis or Kansas City. Brush some Stillhouse Barbecue Sauce on whatever you're grilling near the end of cooking so the sugars will caramelize, but not burn. Everybody will want a little more sauce so serve it warm on the table.

The Meaning of BARBECUE

STILLHOUSE BARBECUE SAUCE

★★★★★★★★★★★★★★★★★★★★★★★★★

1/2 cup grated onion
2 tablespoons oil
1 cup ketchup
1 cup cider vinegar
1 cup Jack Daniel's Tennessee Whiskey
1 cup brown sugar
2 tablespoons Worcestershire sauce
2 tablespoons hot pepper sauce, or to taste

Cook onion in oil in a medium saucepan over medium heat until softened, about 5 minutes. Stir in the remaining ingredients. Bring to a boil, reduce heat, and simmer about 30 minutes, or until slightly thickened. Keep unused portion refrigerated. **Makes about 2 1/2 cups.**

We eat barbecue, we smoke barbecue, but we don't barbecue. Real barbecue is meat cooked slowly and indirectly over a smoldering wood fire, not the act of cooking or the grill itself. In Tennessee and the Southeast, we prefer pork—whole hog, pulled pork butt, or ribs. When cooking a steak or flipping hamburgers over hot coals, to us you're grilling, not barbecuing. The barbecue tradition comes from the days before refrigeration when meats were smoked for preservation and whole hogs were cooked to share with the whole community. Making barbecue is hard work that takes plenty of practice. The South is dotted with barbecue joints and they're not hard to find if you follow your nose and look for a wood pile and smoker out back. These days smoking is a popular backyard pastime. My brother Lee spends his weekends perfecting smoked pork tenderloin, and my friend Randy "Goose" Baxter is famous around here for his smoked turkey breast.

DRY COUNTY DRY RUB

★★★★★★★★★★★★★★★★★★★★★★★★★

1/4 cup paprika
1/4 cup salt
1/4 cup black pepper
1 tablespoon garlic powder

Combine all ingredients in a jar with a tight-fitting lid. Close lid and shake to blend spices. Rub into beef, poultry, pork, or fish before grilling. **Makes about 1 cup.**

NO GRILLER OR PITMASTER'S pantry is complete without a ready batch of easy-to-mix dry rub. My basic batch is nothing more than equal parts salt, pepper, and paprika with a little garlic thrown in. Keep it simple and then customize a small amount for whatever you're cooking. Add some cumin, cayenne, coriander, oregano, onion powder, chili powder, thyme, dried lemon peel, and even cloves. For pork ribs, we add a little sugar. Every Memorial Day weekend, I make a big batch by at least tripling the recipe so we're ready for summer grilling. It keeps forever, but you won't have it that long. Find yourself a good tight-sealing wide-mouth jar.

Jack Daniel's to this basting mix, but I finally realized it was doing me more good in a glass. I first learned about this method of keeping barbecued meats moist while wandering among the barbecue teams at the Jack Daniel's Invitational. Every so often a cooker door would pop open and an arm with a spray bottle attached reached in to douse the pork ribs and butts. Winners swear by it. Mark your spray bottle to be sure you don't use an old bleach sprayer!

Jack Daniel's World Championship
INVITATIONAL BARBECUE

NO JACK CIDER VINEGAR MOPPING SPRAY

★★★★★★★★★★★★★★★★★★★★★★★★★★★★★★★

1 part cider vinegar
2 parts apple cider
1/4 part Worcestershire sauce

Combine ingredients and pour into a clean spray bottle. Spray on barbecue while cooking, as needed, to keep meats moist. For a pork butt or a couple of racks of ribs, make a small batch with 1 cup of vinegar, 2 cups of cider, and 1/4 cup of Worcestershire sauce.

Every year barbecue fans travel to Lynchburg on the fourth Saturday in October for the Jack Daniel's World Championship Invitational Barbecue competition. Since 1988, we've been holding this prestigious contest at the close of barbecue season when the leaves are turning and the air is crisp. It's the ultimate barbecue showdown because in order to qualify, teams must have won a state championship or a competition of more than fifty competitors. Teams from all over the U.S. and the world battle in this exclusive event. We've had folks from Ireland, England, Germany, Australia, Canada, Switzerland, and Japan compete for prizes.

The competition categories are: Pork Ribs, Pork Shoulder, Whole Hog, Beef Brisket, Chicken, Sauce, Dessert.

It's quite a spectacle for town of 500 to host more than 20,000 visitors on one weekend. We all pitch in and volunteer, doing everything from directing traffic to hosting a rolling pin toss to sweeping up on Sunday. Many of our civic organizations plan all year for their biggest fundraising event. Around the courthouse square you'll find the Methodist ladies selling delicious baked goods and homemade fried pies and the volunteer fire department's famous roasted corn. Others are selling fried pork skins and rooster fries.

Beyond the competition, there are lots of fun activities for the whole family. There's a rolling pin toss, butt bowling (pork butts, that is), a country dog contest, and plenty of musical performances on the square, including our local cloggers.

MOJACK FLANK STEAK

★★★★★★★★★★★★★★★★★★★★★★★★★

MOJACK MARINADE

1/4 cup vegetable oil

4 cloves garlic, crushed

1/2 cup Jack Daniel's Tennessee Whiskey

1/2 cup orange juice

1/2 cup fresh lime juice

1 teaspoon ground cumin

1/2 cup soy sauce

STEAKS

2 flank steaks (about 2 pounds each)

Combine all marinade ingredients in a large sealable plastic bag and blend well. Place steaks in the bag and seal. Refrigerate and marinate for at least 1 hour or overnight. Grill steaks directly over high heat about 5 to 7 minutes per side for medium-rare. Remove the steaks from the heat and let rest about 10 minutes before thinly slicing across the grain (slice with the grain for skirt). Serve with tortillas, salsa, and your choice of toppings like chopped tomatoes, onions, avocado slices, lettuce, and jalapeno peppers.

Makes about 2 1/2 cups marinade and 8 servings of steak.

THE POPULARITY OF the Mexican mojo marinades got me thinking about how great those citrus flavors taste with Jack. My Tennessee version works well with beef or chicken. I especially love it on flank or skirt steak for chewy, tender fajitas, and it really perks up those boneless skinless chicken breasts. Serve them all with a big pot of pinto beans and Pepper Jack Rice Bake (see page 101).

secrets at the annual Jack Barbecue competition than the team recipes for sauces, mops, and marinades. I've tasted concoctions using everything from cherry preserves to curry powder to Vietnamese fish sauce. Seems to me the simpler the better. This easy glaze isn't for slow smoked pork barbecue, but it does wonders to perk up grilled meats, poultry, or fish. Brush it on just minutes before you pull the meat off the fire to caramelize, but not burn the sugars. Feel free to add your own "secret ingredient" or two to this basic blend like a little lemon juice, ginger, black pepper, or chili powder. Just don't tell anybody!

OLD NO. 7 TIPS
For Great Grilling

JACK'S ALL-PURPOSE BBQ GLAZE

★★★★★★★★★★★★★★★★★★★★★★★★★★★

1/2 cup Jack Daniel's Tennessee Whiskey
1/2 cup soy sauce
1/2 cup ketchup
1 cup brown sugar
1 teaspoon garlic powder

Combine all ingredients in a small saucepan. Simmer until slightly thickened, about 5 minutes. **Makes about 2 cups.**

Get ready. Preheat the gas grill for a good 10 minutes or fire-up plenty of charcoal and allow 20 to 30 minutes for it to turn to a light grey ash. Keep the grill vents open.

- **Keep it clean.** Scrub grill grates with a wire brush or spatula before and after cooking. Oil the grill grates so food doesn't stick.
- **Season food.** Massage meat, poultry or fish with dry rub before cooking.
- **No piercing.** Use tongs and a spatula to turn food. Piercing with a fork lets out all the precious juices.
- **No water please.** Control flare-ups by moving food away from flames to cooler areas of the grill. Close the grill cover to help cut off oxygen supply.
- **No peeking.** Close the grill cover for even cooking and keep it closed. Test for doneness with an instant read thermometer.
- **Baste late.** Brush sugary sauces on food near the end of cooking to prevent burning.

MASTER DISTILLER'S STEAK WITH JIMMY'S JACK MARINADE

★★★★★★★★★★★★★★★★★★★★★★★★★★★★★★

Jimmy's Jack Marinade

1/2 cup Jack Daniel's Tennessee Whiskey

1/4 cup brown sugar

1/4 cup soy sauce

2 tablespoons Worcestershire sauce

Juice of one lemon

1/4 teaspoon garlic powder

2 1/2 pounds steak of your choice

Combine all marinade ingredients in a large sealable plastic bag, add steaks, and seal. Refrigerate at least 1 hour. Remove the steaks from the marinade and grill over hot coals about 5 minutes per side for medium-rare. **Makes about 1 cup of marinade.**

JACK DANIEL'S MASTER Distiller Jimmy Bedford loves steak more than anyone I know and can stake out the best steak-houses in any town. He's perfected this Jack Marinade and serves it regularly on the back patio surrounded by his wife Emily's gorgeous rose bushes. Use his marinade on any good steak. It makes enough for about 2 1/2 pounds like 2 extra large T-bones or 4 tenderloin fillets.

GRILLED AND GLAZED SALMON

★★★★★★★★★★★★★★★★★★★★★★★★★★★★

2 cloves garlic, minced
2 tablespoons oil
1 tablespoon grated fresh ginger
1/2 cup orange juice
1/4 cup hoisin sauce
1/4 cup Jack Daniel's Tennessee Whiskey
2 tablespoons soy sauce
1 medium orange cut into thin slices, each slice cut in half
4 to 6 salmon steaks or fillets (about 8 ounces each)

Cook garlic in oil in a small saucepan over medium heat until softened, about 2 minutes. Stir in the remaining ingredients except the salmon and bring to a boil. Simmer the sauce about 15 minutes or until slightly thickened. Place salmon on squares of aluminum foil. Grill over medium-high heat with the cover down about 10 minutes. Brush with the glaze and continue to cook 2 to 3 minutes longer or until the fish is cooked through. Serve fish with additional warm sauce spooned over each portion. **Makes 4 to 6 servings.**

ONE OF THE MANY pleasant surprises I've enjoyed while visiting great restaurants across the U.S. and around the globe is how well Jack Daniel's marries with sweet/sour Asian flavors like hoisin sauce, ginger, and soy sauce. This very easy barbecue sauce includes a whole orange (almost like my grand-daddy's barbecue sauce with the whole lemon) called Dad's Barbecue Sauce (see page 122). It works particularly well on meaty salmon steaks or fillets. Serve Icy Pink Cucumbers and Onions (see page 172), a quick colorful vegetable stir fry, and steamed rice on the side.

Hollyhocks are one of my favorite summer flowers. We have a whole bunch growing out back behind the kitchen.

HEARD AROUND
THE TABLE

One of our Tennessee Squires was bragging at the table about owning property at the Distillery. I asked him if he'd brought his lawn mower. He said no, but that he did have tweezers in his pocket.

we all do before bottled Italian dressing and boneless skinless chicken breasts? My unscientific research suggests that a good number of Moore County grillers enjoy the fruits of this now classic combination on a regular basis. For a real kick, add a little Jack and a generous amount of chipotle pepper sauce and use it on any cut-up chicken—with or without bones and skin.

IS IT DONE YET?
Grilling Guidelines for Supper Outside

I-TALIAN GRILLED CHICKEN

★★★★★★★★★★★★★★★★★★★★★★★★★★★

About 2 pounds chicken pieces
1 cup Italian dressing
1/4 to 1/2 cup chipotle pepper sauce
1/4 cup Jack Daniel's Tennessee Whiskey
2 cloves garlic, minced

Place chicken in a sealable plastic bag. Add the remaining ingredients. Refrigerate at least an hour or overnight. Remove the chicken from the marinade and discard the marinade. Grill chicken over medium-high heat until it reaches an internal temperature of 160°F for white meat and 180°F for dark meat. **Makes 6 servings.**

That's the most important question when grilling. A handy instant read thermometer will keep the guesswork to a minimum. Insert the thermometer into the thickest part of the meat without touching any bone. These are the "pull-off-the-grill" temperatures, not final destinations. Remember that all grilled meats continue cooking at least 5 to 10 minutes after they're removed from the heat.

BEEF AND LAMB		POULTRY	
Rare	125°F	White Meat	160°F
Medium-Rare	135°F	Dark Meat	175°F
Medium	145°F		
Well-Done	170°F		

PORK		FISH	
Medium	160°F	Rare	120°F
Well-Done	180°F	Cooked-Through	135°F

TENNESSEE GRILLED QUAIL WITH MOLASSES WHISKEY GLAZE

★★★★★★★★★★★★★★★★★★★★★★★★★★★★★★★

12 whole quail or 6 Cornish game hens, cut in half
Vegetable oil
Salt and pepper
1/2 cup (1 stick) butter
1/2 cup orange juice
1/4 cup Jack Daniel's Tennessee Whiskey
2 tablespoons molasses
1 tablespoon Worcestershire sauce
2 cloves garlic, minced

Rub the birds with oil and sprinkle with salt and pepper. Combine remaining ingredients in a small saucepan. Bring to a boil and simmer until slightly reduced and thickened. Grill the birds over medium heat for 20 to 30 minutes, turning occasionally to brown all sides evenly and crisp the skin. Brush with the glaze during the last 5 minutes of cooking. The birds are cooked when the juices run clear and the internal temperature in the thigh is at least 175° F. **Makes 6 servings.**

QUAIL HUNTING IN Tennessee is really not about the birds, but the beautiful bird dogs raised and trained by many of the hunters around here. Those dogs have endless stamina and an almost magical instinct for deep concentration and stillness. Most hunters will tell you that the best way to enjoy the fruits of a good bird dog is to fry up the quail in a skillet with a side of mashed potatoes, creamy gravy, and a bowlful of tangy slaw. Or, when company's coming, cook the birds outside on a hot grill and lacquer them up with this whiskey molasses glaze. Instead of mashed, roast the potatoes in packets on the grill, but still serve a good creamy slaw.

the commonest thing for dinner in landlocked Middle Tennessee back in Uncle Jack's day. In fact, I don't remember having much shrimp while I was growing up 50 years later, either. But, I imagine if my uncle were alive today, flamboyant party host that he was, spicy fat shrimp would certainly be included on the menu. Serve shrimp skewers as the centerpiece of a meal with Cheese Grits Bake (see page 54) on the side or pass them around to guests as a tasty tidbit with cocktails before the steaks go on the grill. We like them spicy hot with a good dose of pepper sauce.

JACK'S SWEET HOT GLAZED SHRIMP

★★★★★★★★★★★★★★★★★★★★★★★★★★★

2 pounds jumbo shrimp, peeled and deveined with the tails left on
1/4 cup soy sauce
1/4 cup hoisin sauce
2 tablespoons Jack Daniel's Tennessee Whiskey
2 tablespoons brown sugar
2 tablespoons hot pepper sauce, or to taste
2 tablespoons fresh lemon juice
2 cloves garlic, minced

Thread shrimp onto 2 parallel presoaked bamboo or metal skewers. Use about 4 shrimp per skewer. Double skewers make the shrimp more stable and easier to turn while on the grill. Combine the remaining ingredients in a small bowl. Brush shrimp with glaze and grill over medium-hot heat until flesh is opaque, about 3 minutes per side.
Makes 6 servings.

TENNESSEE WHISKEY BURGERS

★★★★★★★★★★★★★★★★★★★★★★★★★★

1 1/2 pounds ground beef
6 slices cheese, optional
6 strips cooked bacon, optional
6 buns or English muffins

SMOKY JACK BURGER SAUCE

3 tablespoons Jack Daniel's Tennessee Whiskey
3 tablespoons Worcestershire sauce
2 teaspoons garlic salt
2 teaspoons liquid smoke

CHILI JACK BURGER SAUCE

3 tablespoons Jack Daniel's Tennessee Whiskey
3 tablespoons Worcestershire sauce
2 teaspoons garlic salt
2 teaspoons chili powder

For either burger recipe, combine all sauce ingredients in a small bowl. Add 3 tablespoons of the whiskey sauce to the ground beef in a large mixing bowl. Blend well with your hands and form into 6 patties. Sear the patties about 2 to 3 minutes per side directly over high heat. Reduce heat to medium or move to a cooler area of the grill. Baste both sides with the remaining sauce and grill until the burgers are cooked through. During the last minutes of cooking, top with cheese and bacon, both optional, and lightly toast the buns or English muffins over medium heat. **Makes 6 servings.**

HERE ARE TWO EASY variations for whiskey burgers that draw raves in my backyard. I like to serve the Smoky Jack burgers open-faced with cheddar cheese and bacon. Instead of the usual soft bun, try a grilled English muffin half. Chili Jack burgers are wonderful with melted pepper Jack cheese and fresh tomato salsa.

do the grilling on our patio. "Well, I knew he couldn't cook," she says. She'd start the charcoal herself and throw on the steaks. When Daddy's cousin Conner Motlow and family came for supper, Mother would always let Conner give her a hand with the steaks. "He'd get the fire so hot and just burnt the fool out of them," Mother remembers fondly. "They'd be charred all the way around but still pink inside." She always served them with a big slab of butter melting on top, baked potatoes, and a congealed salad. These foil-wrapped packet potatoes would have been perfect for Conner's fiery style of grilling.

GRILLED POTATO (AND OTHER VEGETABLE) PACKETS

★★★★★★★★★★★★★★★★★★★★★★★★★★

Red, white, or Yukon Gold waxy potatoes
Olive oil
Salt and pepper, to taste

Cut potatoes into 2-inch chunks. Place about 3 cups of cut potatoes in a single layer on a generous sheet of heavy duty aluminum foil per packet. Drizzle with olive oil and season with salt and pepper. Fold foil around potatoes making a well-sealed packet. Place on the grill over medium heat and cook 15 minutes. Carefully flip the packet and continue to cook until the potatoes are tender, about 20 minutes.
Each packet makes about 4 servings.

Other vegetables that work great in a grill packet are cauliflower, broccoli, brussels sprouts, carrots, and beets.

JACK'S CHAR-GRILLED PEACHES

★★★★★★★★★★★★★★★★★★★★★★★★★★★★★★

1/3 cup brown sugar
1/4 cup melted butter
1/4 cup Jack Daniel's Tennessee Whiskey
4 ripe but firm freestone peaches, halved and pitted

Combine sugar, butter, and Jack Daniel's in a small bowl. Place peaches on a piece of heavy duty aluminum foil and coat all sides with mixture, reserving a couple spoonfuls. Grill peaches cut side down without turning over medium-low heat until lightly charred, about 5 minutes. Turn peaches over and spoon the remaining sugar mixture in the cavities. Continue to cook 2 minutes. Serve with butter pecan or vanilla ice cream. **Makes 4 to 8 servings.**

Uncle Jack and his charred oak barrels inspired me to try this fun trick one day while waiting for the coals to ash over for grilled steaks. Sprinkle a few slices of lemon, orange, or lime with sugar. Grill them quickly over medium heat, just until the sugar melts and caramelizes. The fruit should be lightly charred. Don't worry if you burn a few. Just knock them in the coals and start over. Men particularly enjoy this smoky accent in an icy glass of our Tennessee Whiskey.

FOR THIS SUMPTUOUS grilled fruit dessert, be sure to use "freestone" peaches—the ones that separate easily from the pit. "Clingstone" peaches fight too much and won't look as pretty. If you're serving fish or a saucy meat for supper, grill the peaches on a clean grate beforehand. I slip a piece of aluminum foil between the fruit and the grate to catch the juices. They'll still get plenty charred. Serve them warm or at room temperature. Don't stop with peaches. Try grilling other fruits, like a pineapple cut into 1-inch rings, or banana slices to round out an ice-cream sundae.

COMMON
INGREDIENTS
Charred Fruit for Jack's Highballs

MAYBE IT'S BECAUSE CORN is the main ingredient in Jack Daniel's Tennessee Whiskey that makes me love grilled and roasted corn so much. I know it's showy, but I don't see the need to soak and grill corn wrapped in the husk. Good sweet grilled corn takes only minutes over a hot fire and is an easy side dish with almost any summer-through-fall meal. Heck, these days sweet Florida corn is available all winter long so our grill is busy twelve months of every year. On a rainy day, cook the corn under the broiler until lightly charred on all sides. We always grill more corn than we think we'll need, but rarely have any left over! When we do, I strip it from the cob and add it to salads and casseroles.

SALT AND PEPPERED SWEET CORN

★★★★★★★★★★★★★★★★★★★★★★★★★★★★

8 ears of fresh corn on the cob
1/2 cup (1 stick) butter
Salt and pepper, to taste

Remove husks and silk from corn, but leave the stem intact to use as a handle. Grill corn directly over medium-high heat about 8 to 10 minutes, turning frequently and moving ears around the grate for an evenly browned look. Stay close to the grill—burnt kernels are chewy and tough. Baste with melted butter as corn cooks. Salt, pepper, and eat.

Every October at the Jack Daniel's World Championship Invitational Barbecue competition, follow your nose to the Lynchburg Town Square for the fabulous and famous roasted corn served by our firefighters. Most visitors to the barbecue find out in a hurry that pulled barbecue isn't the only good eating in Lynchburg. At least one smoky ear per person is a necessity during the fall festivities.

JACK IN THE BEANS

★★★★★★★★★★★★★★★★★★★★★★★★★★

2 tablespoons bacon drippings or oil
1 small onion, chopped
2 tablespoons brown sugar
1/3 cup Jack Daniel's Tennessee Whiskey
1 can (28 ounces) baked beans
1 tablespoon spicy brown mustard
2 tablespoons Worcestershire sauce
1/2 teaspoon liquid smoke, optional

Heat drippings in a large saucepan. Stir in the onion and brown sugar.
Cook over medium heat, stirring frequently, until the onion is soft
and golden brown, about 5 minutes. Stir in the remaining ingredients.
Simmer 20 to 30 minutes. **Makes 6 servings.**

AROUND HERE YOU
can't have barbecue, or even a good
grilled hamburger, without beans.
This easy-to-doctor bean recipe
has come in handy more times
than I can remember. Make them
with or without a little smoky flavor
courtesy of liquid smoke, but I always use bacon drippings for added
richness and flavor. Some folks actually put a Dutch oven filled with
beans in the smoker for an hour
or two. Keep the lid ajar to infuse
the beans with real wood flavor.

JACK ONIONS, HONEY?

★★★★★★★★★★★★★★★★★★★★★★★★

4 medium sweet onions (such as Vidalia)
2 tablespoons Jack Daniel's Tennessee Whiskey
4 tablespoons melted butter
1 tablespoon honey
A few fresh sage leaves, optional
Salt and black pepper

Peel onions and cut in half from the top to the bottom. Combine Jack Daniel's, butter, and honey in a small bowl and blend well. Place onions on a large sheet of heavy duty aluminum foil. Drizzle with glaze and sprinkle with sage, salt, and pepper. Fold up and seal the foil packet and roast on the grill over medium heat until tender, about 30 minutes.
Makes 8 servings.

THE ARRIVAL OF SWEET Vidalia onions from Georgia is one of my favorite things about springtime. Some say Vidalias are so sweet you can bite into them just like an apple. I've never tried that, but grilled in a foil packet with a little Tennessee Whiskey, melted butter, and honey they become a classy side dish. Match them with any kind of pork or smoked turkey.

My husband Tom is the football fan, but I'm more of a fan of a good party, even one held in a parking lot. Here's what I've learned on my tailgating trails.

1. **Bring plenty of garbage bags** and paper towels. This is courteous for your group and your neighbors, especially if you plan on tailgating in the same place with the same neighbors regularly.

2. **Grilling is a tailgating tradition,** but if it's not a possibility, there's an endless list of tasty alternatives. How about using your portable propane burner for a big pot of chili or soup, especially when nippy fall weather sets in. I'm also a big sandwich fan. Just be sure to pay attention to your bread and your fillings. The best breads hold up to soggy fillings and the best fillings aren't too soggy to begin with. There's certainly nothing better than good ham biscuits.

3. **Round out the menu with finger foods.** You can't go wrong with pimiento cheese stuffed celery, deviled eggs, and mini muffins. Always bring good chips and toasted nuts for munching. I've also found that folks appreciate a little fresh fruit. Use what's in season like grapes and apples.

4. **A sturdy Thermos or two** will keep drinks and soups hot for hours. Don't forget a Thermos of good hot coffee, either.

5. **Take two coolers**—one for cold drinks filled with plenty of ice and one for food. That way, the host can manage food supplies while the guests can help themselves to drinks. There's nothing worse than icy water seeping into the deviled eggs. Bring plenty of water for drinking and clean-up.

6. **Hot spiced cider** is a great alternative to the usual hot chocolate. Heat it good and hot and add cinnamon sticks. Serve in insulated cups and pass the bottle of Jack Daniel's. Now that will keep everyone warm, even on the chilliest of days.

7. **Bring plenty to share.** At every tailgate occasion, somebody runs out of something. Be a hospitable neighbor and don't hesitate to share. You never know when you'll be the one low on charcoal or paper towels.

Here I am taking Tom for a stroll after another one of his favorite hog jowl breakfasts with Mother!

SWEETS

MOTHER'S HOLIDAY DIVINITY CANDY

★★★★★★★★★★★★★★★★★★★★★★★★★★

AT CHRISTMASTIME, I SO look forward (as does everyone else in Lynchburg) to Mother's Holiday Divinity. Divinity is not the easiest candy to make because success depends on the weather. Mother never makes it on a rainy day (and never in the summertime) because the candy won't firm up in the humidity. She says to wait for a cold and sunny day. A handful of black walnut pieces added to the candy really make it taste like Tennessee. Black walnut trees grow everywhere in Lynchburg, but you can also buy little packets of black walnuts at the grocery store.

3 cups sugar

1/2 cup water

1/2 cup light corn syrup

2 egg whites

1 teaspoon vanilla

1 cup chopped toasted pecans or black walnuts

Combine sugar, water, and corn syrup in a medium saucepan. Bring to a boil over high heat, stirring to dissolve the sugar. Reduce heat and continue to cook without stirring until the syrup reaches 240°F on a candy thermometer.

Beat egg whites until stiff. Slowly pour half of the syrup into the egg whites, beating constantly. Continue to cook the remaining syrup to 265°F on a candy thermometer (hard ball stage). Gradually add it to the egg white mixture. Beat a few minutes more until the fluffy mixture holds its shape when dropped from a spoon. Fold in the vanilla and nuts. Drop by teaspoonfuls onto a greased cookie sheet, working quickly before mixture sets up. Store in an airtight container when firm.

Makes about 24 pieces.

Mother's secrets for perfect divinity every time: If the mixture seems thin and won't hold its shape, sift a little powdered sugar over it while beating. If too thick, boil a little extra water in the saucepan and add it by teaspoonfuls to the mixture while beating to correct the consistency. The only other advice Mother offers is to practice. "Some things take a little experience. Just keep on trying, Honey!" If it still doesn't work, blame it on the weather.

Mother loves the row of windows above the sink where she enjoys her birds and a view of the yard.

HEARD AROUND THE TABLE

I tell folks that oftentimes we substitute Jack Daniel's for vanilla in our cooking so I encourage them to do the same when that pantry staple runs out. One gentleman looked up from his dinner and said, "Honey, I'm gonna run out of Jack Daniel's long before I run out of vanilla."

at Miss Mary's, no one seems to get enough homemade pastry anymore (or any at all). When we serve these apple dumplings completely encased in delicious homemade pastry, you wouldn't believe the moans of delight around the table. Pastry is especially easy to make if you have a pastry cloth, a big square of canvas you store in the freezer for pie crusts and biscuit dough. The flour-coated canvas keeps the dough from sticking so it's easy to roll out. Even better, the kitchen counter stays clean (well, relatively clean).

OLD-FASHIONED APPLE DUMPLINGS

★★★★★★★★★★★★★★★★★★★★★★★★★

APPLE DUMPLINGS

1 recipe for pastry made with 2/3 cup lard (see page 114)
6 medium Golden Delicious or Granny Smith apples
1/2 cup sugar
1 teaspoon cinnamon
3 tablespoons butter, softened

SUGAR SYRUP

1 1/4 cups water
1 tablespoon lemon juice
1/4 cup Jack Daniel's Tennessee Whiskey
3/4 cup sugar
3 tablespoons butter
1 teaspoon cinnamon

Heat the oven to 375°F. Grease a 9 x 13-inch baking dish. Prepare the pastry and divide the dough into 6 equal portions. Roll each ball out into a 7-inch square. Peel and core the apples. Place each apple on a square of pastry. Combine the sugar, cinnamon, and butter in a small bowl. Mix well with a fork. Fill each apple cavity with the sugar mixture. Moisten the edges of the pastry with water. Bring the four corners of the dough up over each apple and seal by pinching and pressing the edges together. Place the apples in the greased baking dish without touching. Bake 15 minutes while you make the sugar syrup.

Combine all the syrup ingredients in a small saucepan. Bring to a boil and simmer about 5 minutes. Pour the hot syrup over and around the apples and continue to bake 30 minutes or until the apples are tender. Spoon some of the syrup over the apples again near the end of baking. Serve with ice cream or whipped cream. **Makes 6 servings.**

LATE-NIGHT OATMEAL CAKE

★★★★★★★★★★★★★★★★★★★★★★★★★★

1 cup rolled oats
1 1/3 cups boiling water
1/2 cup (1 stick) butter, melted
1 cup brown sugar
1 cup sugar
2 eggs
1 1/3 cups all-purpose flour
1 teaspoon baking soda
1/4 teaspoon salt
1 teaspoon cinnamon
1 teaspoon vanilla
Broiled Coconut Pecan Topping (recipe follows)

Heat oven to 350°F. Grease a 9 x 13-inch baking pan. Pour boiling water over the oats in a large mixing bowl and let soften for about 20 minutes. Stir in the remaining ingredients and blend well. Pour into the greased pan. Bake for about 25 to 30 minutes or until sides start to pull away from the pan and the top is golden brown. Spread topping over hot cake. Cook under a hot broiler until the topping is bubbly and lightly browned, about 1 to 2 minutes. **Makes 16 servings.**

BROILED COCONUT PECAN TOPPING

★★★★★★★★★★★★★★★★★★★★★★★★★★★

1/2 cup (1 stick) butter
2 tablespoons milk
1 cup brown sugar
1 cup sweetened shredded coconut
1 cup chopped pecans
1/2 teaspoon vanilla

Melt butter in a small saucepan over medium heat. Stir in the remaining ingredients until well blended. Spread over the hot cake.

W e've been adding Jack Daniel's to recipes that call for vanilla for years because they complement each other so nicely. When we're out of vanilla, we just use Jack by itself. For the best of both worlds, make your own vanilla extract by combining 3 or 4 whole vanilla beans in a pint jar filled with Jack Daniel's Tennessee Whiskey. Seal it tight and leave it to infuse for a few weeks. Use it just as you would store-bought vanilla extract, but know that it's much, much better.

COMMON
INGREDIENTS

Lynchburg vanilla

JACK'S FAMOUS CARAMEL SAUCE

★★★★★★★★★★★★★★★★★★★★★★★★

1/2 cup (1 stick) butter
1 cup brown sugar
1/2 cup heavy cream
1/4 cup Jack Daniel's Tennessee Whiskey

Melt butter in a saucepan over medium heat. Stir in sugar and cream. Bring to a boil, stirring constantly. Remove from heat. Whisk in Jack Daniel's. Serve warm or at room temperature. Cover and keep refrigerated. **Makes about 2 cups.**

JACK'S PUNCHY PEACHES

★★★★★★★★★★★★★★★★★★★★★★★★

2 tablespoons butter
2 cups ripe peeled and sliced fresh peaches (or use 1 bag (12 ounces) frozen sliced peaches)
1/2 cup brown sugar
2 tablespoons Jack Daniel's Tennessee Whiskey
1 teaspoon cornstarch

Melt butter in a medium saucepan. Stir in the peaches and sugar. Cook over medium heat and simmer until sugar dissolves. Combine Jack Daniel's and cornstarch in a small bowl and stir until cornstarch dissolves. Pour into the peaches. Cook, stirring constantly, until slightly thickened and bubbly. Serve warm or at room temperature. Cover and keep refrigerated. **Makes about 2 cups.**

I CAN'T TELL YOU HOW many times any one of these fabulously decadent sauces has gotten me out of a dessert jam. I love any of them over ice cream, but don't stop there. Imagine slices of toasted pound cake and bananas pooled with caramel sauce, layered parfaits with peaches or cherries, brownie sundaes with marshmallow peanut butter sauce, and any apple dessert or bread pudding with the caramel sauce. Broil the brown sugar cream over sweetened fresh fruit in a little oven-proof gratin dish. And what doesn't improve with a little chocolate? When I'm feeling really fancy, I'll make two sauces and mingle them with a dessert.

JACK'S HAPPY CHERRIES

★★★★★★★★★★★★★★★★★★★★★★★★★★★

2 tablespoons butter
2 cans (about 14.5 ounces each) pitted sweet cherries, drained
1/2 cup sugar
1/4 cup Jack Daniel's Tennessee Whiskey
1 tablespoon cornstarch
1/4 teaspoon almond extract

Melt butter in a medium saucepan. Stir in the cherries and sugar. Cook over medium heat and simmer until sugar dissolves. Combine Jack Daniel's and cornstarch in a small bowl and stir until cornstarch dissolves. Stir into the cherries. Cook, stirring constantly, until slightly thickened and bubbly. Stir in almond extract. Serve warm. Cover and keep refrigerated. **Makes 2 1/2 cups.**

JACK'S MARSHMALLOW PEANUT BUTTER SAUCE

★★★★★★★★★★★★★★★★★★★★★★★★★★★

1 jar (7 ounces) marshmallow créme
1/4 cup creamy or crunchy peanut butter
1/4 cup Jack Daniel's Tennessee Whiskey

Combine all ingredients in a small saucepan. Cook, stirring constantly, over medium heat until silky smooth. Serve warm. Cover and keep refrigerated. **Makes about 1 cup.**

JACK'S BEST-EVER FUDGE SAUCE

★★★★★★★★★★★★★★★★★★★★★★★★★★

1 cup heavy cream
1/4 cup Jack Daniel's Tennessee Whiskey
8 ounces good quality semisweet chocolate, cut into small chunks
1/4 cup sugar
1/4 cup light corn syrup

Bring cream and Jack Daniel's to a boil in a saucepan. Remove from heat.
Stir in chocolate, sugar, and corn syrup until smooth and melted. Serve
warm or at room temperature. Cover and keep refrigerated.
Makes about 2 cups.

JACK'S BUTTER MAPLE SAUCE WITH RAISINS

★★★★★★★★★★★★★★★★★★★★★★★★★★

3/4 cup real maple syrup
1/4 cup Jack Daniel's Tennessee Whiskey
2 tablespoons butter
1/2 cup raisins
1 tablespoon fresh orange or lemon zest, optional

Combine all ingredients in a saucepan. Cook over medium heat and
simmer until slightly thickened, about 5 minutes. Stir in a small handful
of toasted pecans or walnuts if you like. **Makes about 1 cup.**

JACK'S BROWN SUGAR CREAM

★★★★★★★★★★★★★★★★★★★★★★★★★★★

1 cup sour cream
1/4 cup brown sugar
2 tablespoons Jack Daniel's Tennessee Whiskey
1/2 teaspoon cinnamon, optional

Combine all ingredients in a small bowl and blend well. Serve with sweetened fresh fruit such as berries, pineapple chunks, or peach slices. **Makes about 1 cup.**

CLASSIC CARAMEL CAKE

★★★★★★★★★★★★★★★★★★★★★★★★★★★

2 cups all-purpose flour
2 teaspoons baking powder
1/4 teaspoon salt
3/4 cup (1 1/2 sticks) butter
1 1/4 cups sugar
6 egg yolks
1 teaspoon vanilla
3/4 cup milk
Caramel Icing (recipe follows)

Heat oven to 375°F. Grease and flour a 9 x 13-inch baking pan. Combine flour, baking powder, and salt in a medium mixing bowl. Cream butter and sugar in a large mixing bowl with an electric mixer. Add egg yolks, one at a time, and beat until light and fluffy. Add vanilla. Gradually blend in the flour alternately with the milk. Beat on medium speed until smooth and creamy, about 2 minutes. Scrape down the sides of the bowl as needed. Pour batter into the greased pan. Bake 25 to 30 minutes or until golden brown and a toothpick inserted in the center comes out clean. Cool and spread with Caramel Icing. **Makes 16 servings.**

MY UNCLE JACK WAS A lively, theatrical man with a big appetite for life, good food, music, and dancing. As Lynchburg's most eligible bachelor and bon vivant, he threw fabulous parties like his annual Second Sunday May dinners, inviting hundreds of folks to his house after church for an all-afternoon feast. The tables would groan with plentiful meats, vegetables, breads and, good gracious, sweets like this traditional caramel cake (my family's favorite). In fact, my nephews John and Conner Tolley absolutely beg Mother for a caramel cake whenever they visit.

CARAMEL ICING

★★★★★★★★★★★★★★★★★★★★★★★★★★

2 1/2 cups sugar, divided
1/2 cup (1 stick) butter
1 egg, lightly beaten
3/4 cup evaporated milk
1 teaspoon vanilla

Heat 1/2 cup of the sugar in a cast-iron skillet over low heat until the sugar melts and begins to turn light brown, about 10 minutes. Stir frequently and watch carefully because the sugar will continue to brown after removing from the heat.

Melt the butter in a large saucepan over medium heat. Stir in the remaining 2 cups of sugar, milk and egg. Bring the mixture to a boil, stirring constantly. Stir in the browned sugar and cook the mixture to the soft ball stage (238°F) on a candy thermometer. Remove from heat, cool to lukewarm and stir in the vanilla. Beat with a wooden spoon or an electric mixer until the icing reaches spreading consistency. If icing gets too thick, add a little more evaporated milk. Spread on cake immediately.

AND, YES, IT'S REALLY all about the icing. You *must* caramelize the sugar in an iron skillet for it to taste just right. But, don't shy away from trying because once you make it, you'll get plenty of requests and opportunities to practice!

HEARD AROUND THE TABLE

When a California man reached for his camera a fellow guest offered to take his photograph. The California man replied, "No, thanks. I just want to take a picture of my *plate!* They'll never believe this back home." Later he said that if he ever had the misfortune to find himself on death row his last meal would be a dinner plate from Miss Mary's.

pie recipe at Miss Mary's. A good fudge pie surely satisfies any chocoholic's cravings and proves once and for all that an old-fashioned recipe can stand up to any fancy flourless chocolate torte any day of the week. Folks are always so surprised when they see how easy it is to make. It certainly deserves a big dollop of whipped cream kissed with a little Jack.

MISS MARY'S FUDGE PIE

★★★★★★★★★★★★★★★★★★★★★★★★★

1/4 cup (1/2 stick) butter
1 1/2 cups sugar
3 tablespoons cocoa powder
2 eggs, beaten
1/2 cup evaporated milk
1 tablespoon Jack Daniel's Tennessee Whiskey
1 (9-inch) graham cracker pie crust
Sweetened whipped cream

Heat oven to 350°F. Melt butter in a saucepan over medium heat. Stir in sugar and cocoa powder. Stir in eggs, evaporated milk, and Jack Daniel's. Pour into the prepared pie crust and bake for 30 to 35 minutes or until set. Cool completely. Serve slices with a dollop of whipped cream sweetened with sugar and a little Jack Daniel's. Sprinkle cream with a dusting of cocoa powder. **Makes 8 servings**

cake a few years back to serve at Jack's 150th birthday celebrations all around the country. You can make it in a tube pan for looks, but I prefer a trusty old 9 x 13-inch baking pan because it's easier to tote around and perfect for cutting into neat squares.

JACK'S BIRTHDAY CAKE

★★★★★★★★★★★★★★★★★★★★★★★★★

2 1/4 cups all-purpose flour
2 1/4 teaspoons baking powder
1/2 teaspoon salt
1 cup (2 sticks) butter
2 cups firmly packed brown sugar
4 eggs
1/2 cup Jack Daniel's Tennessee Whiskey
1 cup chopped pecans
1 package (6 ounces) semisweet chocolate chips
Hot Buttered Whiskey Glaze (recipe follows)

CONTINUED ON NEXT PAGE

★★★★★★★★★★★★★★★★★★★★★★★★★★★★★★★★★★

Heat oven to 325°F. Grease a 9 x 13-inch baking pan. Combine the flour, baking powder, and salt in a medium mixing bowl. Set aside. Melt butter in a large saucepan over low heat. Remove from heat. Stir in the brown sugar, eggs, flour mixture, and Jack Daniel's, stirring well after each addition. Pour batter into the greased pan. Sprinkle evenly with pecans and chocolate chips. Bake 45 to 50 minutes or until center of the cake is firm and edges begin to pull away from the sides of the pan. Cool on a wire rack and drizzle with glaze. **Makes 16 servings.**

Cake may be baked in a greased 10-inch tube pan. Increase the baking time to 1 hour. Cool in the pan 10 minutes. Turn out onto a wire rack and cool completely. Drizzle with the glaze.

HOT BUTTERED WHISKEY GLAZE

★★★★★★★★★★★★★★★★★★★★★★★★★★★★

1/4 cup melted butter
2 cups powdered sugar
3 tablespoons Jack Daniel's Tennessee Wiskey
1 teaspoon vanilla

Combine all ingredients in a small bowl. Blend well with a wooden spoon. Drizzle over the cake.

of Bananas Foster is named in honor of my Uncle Dale's father, Herb Fanning, who lived well into his nineties and always said he was so old that he never bought green bananas. Herbie's face may be familiar to you as he appeared in more Jack Daniel's ads than anyone else. On your next visit to Lynchburg, be sure to notice the life-size bronze statue of Herbie sitting at his beloved checkerboard in front of the Hardware Store. Take a minute and have your picture made with him.

FLAMING JACK
What Everyone Should Know about Flaming a Dish

BANANAS FANNING

★★★★★★★★★★★★★★★★★★★★★★★★★★

1/4 cup (1/2 stick) butter
1 cup pecan halves
4 bananas, sliced
1/2 cup brown sugar
Pinch of nutmeg
1/2 cup Jack Daniel's Tennessee Whiskey
Vanilla ice cream

Melt butter in a large skillet. Stir in the pecans and bananas. Cook over medium-low heat, about 3 minutes. Stir in sugar and nutmeg and cook until sugar dissolves, about 2 minutes. Stir in Jack Daniel's and heat until bubbly. Carefully ignite the edge of the pan with a match. Serve warm spooned over vanilla ice cream. **Makes 6 servings.**

Flaming or flambéing is simply a dish set to fire by igniting a small amount of liquor poured over it. It's a good skill to have because you never know when you may need to perform a showy display of dancing blue flames. It's easy to do and all kinds of foods can be flamed, from smoky cocktail wieners to classic Bananas Foster. Here's how:

The first word is caution. Remember you're playing with fire. Keep your face, body, clothing and anything else flammable away from your work area and the flames.

You need heat. The food to be ignited should be warm. The Jack used to ignite the food must also be warm—but not boiling hot. Heat the whiskey after adding to the surface of the food to be ignited just to the point when the alcohol starts to vaporize and steam. Then it's ready to flame. Ignite by touching the edge of the pan to a flame (a long-handled match or lighter). The flames will die down by themselves in a short time.

Practice.

Here's the bronze statue of Herb Fanning waiting for his next checkers opponent. Herb was one of Lynchburg's most recognizable gentlemen, thanks to Jack Daniel's advertisements.

pumpkin pie next Thanksgiving after a taste of this cake. In fact, you may start hearing requests for pumpkin birthday cake as well. Reliable canned pumpkin puree makes this cake exceptionally moist and tender. I often find that many pumpkin pies and cakes overdo the spices to the point of bitterness. You'll find this one refreshingly pure and perfect with just a hint of Jack Daniel's and cinnamon.

PUMPKIN PATCH SQUARES

★★★★★★★★★★★★★★★★★★★★★★★★

2 cups self-rising flour
2 cups sugar
2 teaspoons cinnamon
4 eggs, beaten
1 cup oil
2 cups pumpkin puree
2 tablespoons Jack Daniel's Tennessee Whiskey
2 teaspoons vanilla
Cinnamon Cream Cheese Frosting (recipe follows)

Heat oven to 350°F. Grease a 9 x 13-inch baking pan. Combine flour, sugar, and cinnamon in a large mixing bowl. Stir in eggs, oil, pumpkin, Jack Daniel's, and vanilla until smooth. Pour the batter into the greased baking pan. Bake 30 to 35 minutes or until lightly browned, firm on the top, and the edges begin to pull away from the sides of the pan. Cool and spread with Cinnamon Cream Cheese Frosting. **Makes 16 servings.**

CINNAMON CREAM CHEESE FROSTING

★★★★★★★★★★★★★★★★★★★★★★★★

1 package (8 ounces) cream cheese, softened
1/4 cup (1/2 stick) butter
1 tablespoon Jack Daniel's Tennessee Whiskey
2 teaspoons vanilla
1/2 teaspoon cinnamon
1 box (16 ounces) powdered sugar

Cream the cream cheese and butter in a large mixing bowl with an electric mixer until light and fluffy. Add the Jack Daniel's, vanilla, and cinnamon. Gradually blend in the sugar until thick and creamy. Spread on the cooled cake.

TOWN SQUARE CHESS SQUARES

★★★★★★★★★★★★★★★★★★★★★★★★★★★★★

1 cup butter
2 cups brown sugar
1/2 cup sugar
4 eggs
1 teaspoon vanilla
2 cups all-purpose flour
1 teaspoon baking powder
1/2 teaspoon salt
1 cup chopped pecans
Jack's Whiskey Buttermilk Butterscotch Sauce (recipe follows)

Heat oven to 350°F. Grease a 9 x 13-inch baking pan. Cream butter and sugars in a large mixing bowl until fluffy. Add eggs and vanilla, beating until smooth. Blend in the flour, baking powder, and salt. Stir in the pecans. Pour into the greased pan. Bake for 25 to 30 minutes or until just set. Cool. Cut into squares and serve with a spoonful of Jack's Whiskey Buttermilk Butterscotch Sauce (made without the pecans). **Makes 16 servings. Or cut them into 24 smaller bar cookie portions.**

JACK'S WHISKEY BUTTERMILK BUTTERSCOTCH SAUCE

★★★★★★★★★★★★★★★★★★★★★★★★★★★★★

1 cup sugar
1/2 cup buttermilk
1/2 cup (1 stick) butter
2 tablespoons corn syrup
2 tablespoons Jack Daniel's Tennessee Whiskey
1 cup toasted chopped pecans, optional

CONTINUED ON NEXT PAGE

square anchors our beautiful town and serves as the seat of Tennessee's tiniest county, Moore County. Life revolves around the square with its quaint shops and local businesses that serve our needs and welcome the thousands of folks who visit us each year. Take a stroll around and you'll feel right at home.

These rich chess squares are often at the center of Miss Mary's dessert of the day. Let's just say they're utterly rich and sugary, and if that's not enough, they're topped with Jack's Whiskey Buttermilk Butterscotch Sauce. Trust me, one square and you'll need to take another stroll!

★★★★★★★★★★★★★★★★★★★★★★★★★

Combine sugar, buttermilk, and butter in a small saucepan. Cook, stirring constantly, and simmer until the sugar has melted and the mixture is smooth. Stir in Jack Daniel's and nuts. Serve warm or at room temperature. Cover and keep refrigerated.
Makes about 3 cups with nuts.

TENNESSEE TRUFFLES
★★★★★★★★★★★★★★★★★★★★★★★★★

1/2 cup heavy cream
8 ounces good quality semisweet chocolate, coarsely chopped
2 tablespoons Jack Daniel's Tennessee Whiskey
Unsweetened cocoa powder

Bring the cream to a boil in a saucepan over medium heat. Combine the hot cream and the chocolate in a medium bowl, stirring until the chocolate has melted. Add the Jack Daniel's and stir until smooth. Cover and refrigerate until slightly firm. Form into bite-size balls and roll each in cocoa powder. Store the truffles in an airtight container in the refrigerator. Before serving, let them sit at room temperature about 30 minutes to soften. **Makes about 25 to 30.**

ITALIAN CREAM CAKE

★★★★★★★★★★★★★★★★★★★★★★★★★

1/2 cup shortening
1/2 cup (1 stick) butter, softened
2 cups sugar
5 eggs, separated
1 teaspoon vanilla
2 cups all-purpose flour
1 teaspoon baking soda
1/4 teaspoon salt
1 cup buttermilk
1 1/2 cups shredded sweetened or thawed frozen coconut
1 cup chopped pecans
Cream Cheese Icing (recipe follows)

Heat oven to 350°F. Grease a 9 x 13-inch pan. Cream the shortening, butter, and sugar in a large mixing bowl with an electric mixer until light and fluffy. Add egg yolks and vanilla and beat well. In another bowl, stir together the flour, baking soda, and salt. Blend in flour alternately with the buttermilk until smooth. In another mixing bowl, beat the egg whites until stiff and gently fold them into the batter. Stir in the coconut and pecans. Bake 35 minutes or until golden brown on top and a toothpick inserted in the center comes out clean. Spread with Cream Cheese Icing. **Makes 16 to 24 servings.**

Quick Coconut Cake: Omit the nuts in the Italian Cream Cake. After the cake has baked and cooled slightly, poke holes in the top with a skewer or toothpick. Pour 1 can (8.5 ounces) of cream of coconut over the cake. Cool completely and frost with Cream Cheese Icing or sweetened whipped cream. Sprinkle the top with 1 cup shredded sweetened or thawed frozen coconut.

I'VE NEVER UNDERSTOOD why this cake, so popular in the South, is called "Italian." It's certainly not the buttermilk, pecans, and coconut, or the cream cheese icing! Geographical references aside, it's really delicious. Most folks can't help but sneak seconds. Mother prefers a traditional Tennessee coconut cake made only with fresh coconut and without the nuts. Regrettably, time and two seatings a day at Miss Mary's don't always allow such purity. Try my quick cheater version at the bottom of this recipe (even Mother likes it.)

CREAM CHEESE ICING

★★★★★★★★★★★★★★★★★★★★★★★★★★★★★

1 package (8 ounces) cream cheese, softened
1/4 cup (1/2 stick) butter
1 box (16 ounces) powdered sugar
1 teaspoon vanilla

Combine cream cheese and butter in a medium mixing bowl. Beat with an electric mixer until smooth. Add sugar and vanilla and beat until creamy and smooth.

MOTHER'S SUGAR BOX POUND CAKE

★★★★★★★★★★★★★★★★★★★★★★★★★★★★★

1 1/2 cups (3 sticks) butter
1 box (16 ounces) powdered sugar
Juice of one lemon (about 2 tablespoons)
1 teaspoon almond extract
1/2 teaspoon vanilla
1/4 teaspoon salt
1 powdered sugar box (about 4 cups) cake flour
6 eggs

Heat oven to 300°F. Grease and flour a 10-inch tube pan. Cream the butter and sugar in a large mixing bowl with an electric mixer until light and fluffy. Blend in the lemon juice, almond extract, vanilla, and salt. Measure the flour by lightly spooning it into the empty powdered sugar box. Gradually add the flour to the batter alternating with the eggs. Beat well with an electric mixer after each addition until batter is light and fluffy. Pour the batter into the greased pan. Bake 1 hour and 15 minutes or until golden brown and a toothpick inserted in the center comes out clean. **Makes 16 servings.**

MOTHER ALWAYS SAYS, "I'm a butter cook!" This real butter pound cake kept homesickness at bay for my brother and me while we were away at school. All our friends loved it when a fresh-baked care-package arrived from Lynchburg. You haven't lived until you've tasted a slice of this rich cake, buttered and toasted, with a good hot cup of coffee for breakfast. If you think the cake batter needs some milk, Mother says, "No, I haven't forgotten the liquid. You don't use any in this cake!"

SOUTHERN SHORTCAKE

★★★★★★★★★★★★★★★★★★★★★★★★★

2 cups self-rising flour
3 tablespoons sugar
1/2 cup (1 stick) butter, cut into small pieces
3/4 cup milk

Heat oven to 450°F. Combine flour and sugar in a medium mixing bowl. Cut in butter with a pastry blender or two knives until the mixture resembles coarse crumbs. Add milk and stir just until a soft dough forms. Knead the dough on a lightly floured surface or pastry cloth until smooth, about 10 times. Roll out dough to 1/2-inch thickness. Cut with a floured cutter or into squares with a knife. Place on a baking sheet about 1 inch apart. Bake about 10 minutes or until golden brown. Split and butter the shortcakes. Fill and top with sweetened fruit and whipped cream. **Makes 10 to 12 shortcakes.**

Pastry Shortcake: Prepare the pastry (see page 114). Roll out the dough to about 1/8-inch thick. Cut into 3-inch squares or circles. Arrange on a large baking sheet. Bake at 425°F for about 10 minutes. Cool. Layer sweetened fruit and whipped cream between two pieces of pastry. Top with additional fruit and cream.

WE SERVE A RICH BISCUIT shortcake at Miss Mary's in the late spring and summer when fresh peaches and berries are abundant and sweet. Biscuit shortcake is wonderful, but Mother prefers to make hers with circles of crisp baked pastry. Pastry layered with sweetened berries and real whipped cream is a wonderful contrast of flavors and textures and is probably my favorite summer dessert. You can make shortcake with any biscuit, but here the recipe calls for butter instead of lard or shortening and a touch of sugar. Serve the fruit blended with enough sugar to combat the tartness and let the mixture sit at room temperature for the flavors and juices to develop before serving. Yes, you can splash in a tablespoon or two of Jack Daniel's.

with pastry, but this easy drop biscuit version is a close second. If you don't have an iron or oven-proof skillet, pour the warm fruit into a greased 9 x 13-inch baking dish before topping with the dumplings. Mother and I especially like a combination of blackberries and peaches, but one or the other alone is fine, too. Taste the fruit mixture and add sugar accordingly.

MOTLOW SKILLET COBBLER

★★★★★★★★★★★★★★★★★★★★★★

FRUIT

1/4 cup (1/2 stick) butter

1 cup sugar

1/3 cup Jack Daniel's Tennessee Whiskey

3 tablespoons all-purpose flour

10 cups sliced, peeled fresh peaches and blackberries

DUMPLINGS

2 cups self-rising flour

1/4 cup sugar

3/4 cup milk

5 tablespoons butter, melted

1/2 teaspoon vanilla

Heat oven to 425°F. Melt the butter in a 12-inch cast-iron skillet. Stir in sugar, Jack Daniel's, and flour; blend well. Stir in the fruit and simmer over medium-low heat while preparing the dumplings.

Combine the flour and sugar in a medium mixing bowl. Stir in the milk, butter, and vanilla just until a soft dough forms. Drop by tablespoonfuls over the warm fruit. Bake about 15 minutes or until the dumplings are lightly browned. Serve warm or at room temperature with ice cream, whipped cream, or drizzled with heavy cream. **Makes 10 to 12 servings.**

JD BREAD PUDDING

★★★★★★★★★★★★★★★★★★★★★★★★★

1 cup raisins
1 tablespoon fresh orange or lemon zest
1/3 cup Jack Daniel's Tennessee Whiskey
7 cups cubed white bread, lightly toasted
4 eggs
1 cup sugar
3 cups milk
1 teaspoon vanilla
1/4 cup (1/2 stick) butter, cut into small pieces
Nutmeg, to taste

Combine the raisins, zest, and Jack Daniel's in a small bowl. Let soak about 20 minutes. Butter a 9 x 13-inch baking dish. Place bread cubes in the prepared dish. Whisk together the eggs and sugar in a large mixing bowl. Stir in the milk and vanilla. Sprinkle the raisin mixture evenly over the bread cubes. Pour the egg mixture over the bread and let stand about 15 minutes. Heat the oven to 375°F. Dot the top of the pudding with butter and sprinkle with nutmeg. Bake until golden brown and set in the center, about 35 to 40 minutes. Serve warm. Drizzle each serving with heavy cream, if desired. **Makes 12 servings.**

I GET REGULAR REQUESTS for a great bread pudding recipe spirited with Jack Daniel's and here it is. Few things can top whiskey-soaked raisins and I'm especially fond of the fresh orange or lemon zest zing. Always use good quality white bread. Miss Mary's boarder Ruth Hall, a former Moore County extension agent and Miss Mary's table hostess, even made her bread pudding with leftover homemade biscuits. Dee likes the nutmeg in this one and you know she adds a little extra when no one is watching.

was a convenient way for rural Tennessee homemakers to flavor and sweeten a dessert out of season. Traditional Tennessee jam cake is often made with blackberry jam that gives it an unusual purplish hue. For years Mother has been making my grandmother's towering old-fashioned three-layered jam cake that requires all afternoon in the kitchen. This handy 9 x 13-inch version retains the cake's traditional flavor (and funny color), but simplifies the cake batter. I've even streamlined the icing with a luscious Brown Sugar Whiskey Icing instead of traditional caramel.

EASY MADE JAM CAKE

★★★★★★★★★★★★★★★★★★★★★★★★★★

3 eggs
1 1/2 cups brown sugar
1 cup vegetable oil
1 cup seedless blackberry jam
1/2 cup buttermilk
2 1/2 cups self-rising flour
1 teaspoon cinnamon
1/2 teaspoon cloves
1/2 teaspoon nutmeg
1 cup chopped pecans, black walnuts, or walnuts
Brown Sugar Whiskey Icing (recipe follows)

Heat oven to 350°F. Beat the eggs in a large mixing bowl. Stir in the brown sugar, vegetable oil, jam, and buttermilk. Blend well. Stir in the flour, cinnamon, cloves, and nutmeg, beating until smooth. Fold in the nuts. Pour into the greased baking pan. Bake 30 to 35 minutes or until the sides begin to pull away from the pan and the top is firm and lightly browned. Let cool and frost with Brown Sugar Whiskey Icing.

BROWN SUGAR WHISKEY ICING

★★★★★★★★★★★★★★★★★★★★★★★★★★

1/2 cup (1 stick) butter
1/2 cup brown sugar
3 tablespoons milk
2 tablespoons Jack Daniel's Tennessee Whiskey
1 teaspoon vanilla
2 cups powdered sugar

CONTINUED ON NEXT PAGE

Melt the butter in a saucepan over medium heat. Stir in the brown sugar, milk, and Jack Daniel's and bring to a boil. Cook and stir the mixture until thickened and bubbly, about 2 minutes. Remove the pan from the heat. Stir in the vanilla and sugar. Beat with a wooden spoon until smooth and spreadable. Spread over the cooled jam cake.

BOBO'S MACAROON PIE

★★★★★★★★★★★★★★★★★★★★★★★★★★

3 egg whites
1 cup sugar
1 teaspoon almond extract
12 saltine crackers, finely crushed
1/4 teaspoon baking powder
1/3 cup chopped dates
1/2 cup sliced almonds or chopped pecans, toasted

Heat oven to 350°F. Grease a 9-inch pie pan. Beat egg whites until frothy in a large mixing bowl with an electric mixer. Gradually beat in the sugar until the egg whites are stiff and glossy. Add the almond extract. Fold in the cracker crumbs and baking powder. Fold in the dates and nuts. Spoon the mixture into the pie plate. Bake 25 to 30 minutes. The top will look golden brown and crisp. Cool before serving. Serve with sweetened fresh fruit and whipped cream. **Makes 6 servings.**

THE SURPRISE INGREDIENT in this macaroon pie is cracker crumbs that magically disappear while the meringue bakes. The pie is light and crisp and absolutely sumptuous with seasonal fruits. Our local Tennessee peaches are especially nice with the flavor of almond. I think almond extract adds an exotic taste to desserts and Mother refuses to bake a pound cake without it. In winter, she shares her special cranberry sauce, usually reserved for biscuits, with this out-of-the-ordinary dessert. Instead of fruits, generous spoonfuls of whipped cream and tart lemon curd, homemade or from a jar, is exceptionally luscious, stylish, and simple.

The Jack Daniel
DISTILLERY TOUR

Established in the 1830s and registered with the U.S. Government in 1866 by Jack Daniel, the Jack Daniel Distillery is the oldest registered distillery in the United States (registered No. 1). The Distillery is also listed on the National Register of Historic Places.

Jasper Newton (Jack) Daniel was a life-long resident of Lynchburg and the founder of the Distillery. Long ago he proclaimed "Every day we make it, we make it the best we can." We still make it his way and the best we can, too.

Every year roughly 250,000 people from around the world visit Lynchburg and tour the Distillery. The Distillery offers guided tours, free of charge, 9 a.m. through 4:30 p.m. seven days a week, except Thanksgiving Day, Christmas Day, and New Year's Day. All you do is stop by the Visitors Center and sign up for the next tour.

It'll take you about an hour to see our Distillery. You'll see every step we take to make our Tennessee Whiskey. You'll meet plenty of friendly people who are glad to see you and proud to include you in our lives here in Lynchburg. Mother says Lynchburg is the best place in the world to live because folks are friendly and everyone helps each other out.

HIGHLIGHTS OF THE JACK DANIEL DISTILLERY TOUR

- **You'll see the rickyard** where cords of hard sugar maple wood are burned to make the famous charcoal used to mellow the whiskey drop by drop.
- **You'll see the underground cave spring**, the source of the iron-free water necessary for making our whiskey. The water runs at a constant 56°F.
- **You can take your picture** next to our life-size bronze statue of Mr. Jack where he stands near the Cave Spring, at his historic white marble statue in the Visitors Center, or even in Jack Daniel's first office which bears the plaque designating the Distillery as a National Historic Register site.
- **You'll see the whole whiskey-making process,** including the whiskey stills, the fermenting tanks filled with only the finest corn, rye and barley malt, and the charcoal-mellowing vats where whiskey drips through the charcoal over a ten-day process. This special charcoal mellowing helps produce the smoothness and flavor characteristics that make Jack Daniel's a Tennessee Whiskey.

- **You'll see a barrel house** where the whiskey is aged for four years. Barrel houses store more than 20,000 barrels of whiskey, each holding about 50 gallons and weighing more than 400 pounds. Just about everywhere you look you'll see barrel houses dotting the hillsides around Lynchburg.
- **You'll see the White Rabbit Saloon,** a reconstruction of a saloon Uncle Jack operated in Lynchburg before Prohibition. There, we'll serve you a glass of lemonade or coffee and you can visit the little shop that sells commemorative bottles of Jack Daniel's Tennessee Whiskey, the only place in Moore County where whiskey is sold.
- **Be sure to visit our beautiful town square**—just a short walk from the Distillery—where there are a variety of local merchants and shops including the Lynchburg Jail that's now a museum. The Lynchburg Hardware and

Here's where you'll start your Distillery tour next time you come see us. The Visitors Center is down the street from Miss Mary's. Just stop in and sign up for the next tour.

General Store, originally opened by Jack Daniel's nephew, Lem Motlow, so he could make a living during Prohibition, offers the whole line of Jack Daniel's merchandise. There's the Tennessee Walking Horse Museum and the Barrel Shop that sells all kinds of furniture and creative household items crafted from used Jack Daniel's oak barrels.

- **The centerpiece of our town square** is our red brick courthouse (Lynchburg is the county seat) built in 1884 from brick made right here in Moore County. Miss Mary's is just a few houses down from the square.
- **You can also visit the Lynchburg cemetery** and see my Uncle Jack's grave. Look for the two cast-iron chairs originally placed by the grave for local ladies who mourned the passing of Lynchburg's most eligible bachelor.
- **Lynchburg** is halfway between Interstate 65 and Interstate 24 about 75 miles south of Nashville, Tennessee.

RELISHES &
LITTLE EXTRAS

LYNCHBURG CRANBERRY RELISH is the most unfussy accent we serve during the holidays. It tastes great as is or use it as a starting point for your own creative additions. Consider chunks of fresh pineapple, chopped toasted pecans or walnuts, chopped fresh apples and pears, and a sprinkling of cinnamon. I've seen it with horseradish, pistachio nuts, onion, and chopped figs. Be sure to chill the relish overnight for the flavors to really meld. Mother loves a cooked cranberry sauce simply made of cranberries, sugar, and water. Simmer the berries just until they begin to pop, about five minutes. Her freezer is never without a container or two of this luscious red sauce that she particularly enjoys with warm biscuits in the morning.

WARM GRILLED MEATS BEG FOR THE crisp tangy bite of these cold pickled onions and cucumbers. The muted pastel palette of red onions turned pink by a vinegar bath with transluscent cucumber slices and the creeping heat of jalapenos adds a bright crunch to a picnic table filled with traditional creamy summer salads. Adjust the sugar level to your liking. An inexpensive plastic mandoline or V-slicer makes perfect paper thin cucumber slices in seconds. Serve it in a clear glass bowl to show off the spectacular colors and shapes.

LYNCHBURG CRANBERRY RELISH

★★★★★★★★★★★★★★★★★★★★★★

4 cups fresh cranberries
1 whole orange, quartered, seeds removed
2 cups sugar
1/4 cup Jack Daniel's Tennessee Whiskey

Chop cranberries and orange in a food processor. Add sugar and process just to combine. Place in a covered container and chill overnight. Add Jack Daniel's just before serving. **Makes about 5 cups.**

ICY PINK CUCUMBERS AND ONIONS

★★★★★★★★★★★★★★★★★★★★★★

1 large red onion, cut into quarters, then into very thin wedges
2 large or three medium cucumbers, peeled and thinly sliced
3 jalapeno peppers, seeded and thinly sliced
2 cups distilled vinegar
2 to 4 tablespoons sugar
1 tablespoon salt

Combine all ingredients in a medium bowl. Blend well. Cover with plastic wrap, pressing the vegetables into the brine. Refrigerate overnight. Serve cold. **Makes 6 cups.**

TANGY TOMATO ONION RELISH

★★★★★★★★★★★★★★★★★★★★

1/4 cup golden raisins

1/4 cup Jack Daniel's Tennessee Whiskey

3 large sweet onions (like Vidalia), coarsely chopped
(about 6 cups)

2 tablespoons oil

1 tablespoon brown sugar

1 can (14.5 ounces) diced tomatoes, drained

Pinch of thyme

Salt and pepper, to taste

Combine raisins and Jack Daniel's in small bowl; set aside to soak. Cook onion in oil in a large skillet over medium-low heat until tender and golden brown, about 15 minutes, stirring occasionally. Stir in brown sugar and continue to cook 5 minutes. Stir in tomatoes, raisins, and Jack Daniel's. Bring to a boil. Reduce heat and simmer 10 minutes or until thickened. Season with thyme, and salt and pepper. Cool, cover, and refrigerate. Serve chilled or at room temperature. **Makes about 2 1/2 cups.**

RAISINS IN A TOMATO ONION RELISH recipe might surprise you, but plumped with a little Jack Daniel's, they're just right. Grilled pork tenderloin simply begs for a little side of this relish, especially when thinly sliced on soft rolls for tailgating and cocktail parties. Be sure to cook the onions long and slow to develop their sweet flavor.

HEARD AROUND THE TABLE

Forty Australian teachers were asked by their Knoxville teacher friends what they knew about Tennessee so they could figure out how to entertain them during their visit. They knew four things: Dolly Parton, Elvis Presley, Tennessee Walking Horses, and Jack Daniel.

inexpensive, and no one knew that better than Miss Mary. In her day, when times were tight, cabbage appeared in dish after dish, from casseroles to slaws to relishes. Recalling her days in Miss Mary's kitchen, Dee tells about the many times when Miss Mary's phone would ring with pleas from the Distillery to add a few extra table settings for hungry guests. "We'd just about throw a fit, scared we'd run out of food." Miss Mary would strut into the kitchen like a mother hen with her hands up under her arms and holler, "Just stretch it!" One more cabbage dish often saved dinner, even if slaw, kraut and wieners, and boiled cabbage were already on the table!

NOT A DAY PASSES AT MISS MARY'S that a guest doesn't inquire about this recipe. Whenever a bean dish is on the menu, which is most days, diners generously spoon this crimson sweet-savory relish atop their speckled butter beans, pintos, white beans, crowder or black-eyed peas. We find it easiest to chop the peppers and onions uniformly in a food processor.

CAVE SPRING CABBAGE RELISH

★★★★★★★★★★★★★★★★★★

4 cups finely chopped cabbage (about 1/2 a head, or 1
  bag of prepared chopped cabbage for slaw)
1 medium green bell pepper, chopped
1 cup chopped celery
1 jar (4 ounces) chopped pimientos
1/4 cup brown sugar
1/4 cup cider vinegar
1 teaspoon salt
1/2 teaspoon celery seed
1/2 teaspoon whole mustard seed

Combine cabbage, bell pepper, celery, and pimientos in a large bowl. Combine sugar, vinegar, and seasonings in a separate small bowl and pour over the cabbage mixture. Blend well. Chill before serving. **Makes about 5 cups.**

EVERYDAY SWEET RED PEPPER RELISH

★★★★★★★★★★★★★★★★★★

2 cups cider vinegar
2 cups sugar
2 tablespoons tomato paste
6 large red bell peppers, cored, seeded and finely chopped
2 medium onions, finely chopped
2 teaspoons salt
2 teaspoons whole mustard seed
1 teaspoon whole celery seed
A pinch of crushed red pepper

CONTINUED ON NEXT PAGE

★★★★★★★★★★★★★★★★★★★★★★★★★★★

Combine vinegar, sugar, and tomato paste in a large saucepan. Bring to a boil. Add peppers, onions, and seasonings. Simmer about 30 minutes. Cool, cover tightly, and refrigerate. If you're a canner, seal in 1/2 pint or pint jars. **Makes 8 cups.**

BLACK AND BLUE CHEESE BUTTER

★★★★★★★★★★★★★★★★★★★★★★★★★

1/2 cup (1 stick) butter, softened
1/4 cup crumbled blue cheese
1 tablespoon Jack Daniel's Tennessee Whiskey
1 tablespoon finely chopped fresh parsley
1 tablespoon finely chopped fresh chives

Combine all ingredients in a small bowl. Blend well with a wooden spoon. Roll mixture into a 1 1/2-inch diameter cylinder shape in a piece of waxed paper. Refrigerate until firm. Slice and place a pat of the butter on slices of warm grilled steak or serve with baked sweet potatoes.
Makes about 3/4 cup.

BLACK AND BLUE CHEESE BUTTER melting over a juicy grilled steak is a blessed culinary union, but that's not the only happy marriage of flavors. You might be surprised to see how easily this compound butter can make a sophisticated side dish out of a simple baked sweet potato. Instead of the usual brown sugar and marshmallows, the contrasting flavor of creamy, savory blue cheese only makes sweet potatoes sweeter. Try this once and you'll be hooked.

Sour Orange Cherry Sauce with panfried thin scallops of pounded pork tenderloin dredged in flour. Toss all the ingredients into the skillet with the drippings and serve warm with the meat. If you're grilling, make a batch in a small saucepan. Lynchburg duck hunters also love this sauce, so unless you hunt or know a generous hunter with a full freezer, hunt down a duck in your supermarket.

is delicious on every kind of baked winter squash, baked sweet potatoes, and plain old carrots. For breakfast, leave out the Worcestershire sauce and salt and spread it on hot biscuits. A tablespoon of fresh orange zest adds a nice citrus touch.

SWEET AND SOUR ORANGE CHERRY SAUCE

★★★★★★★★★★★★★★★★★★★★

1/2 cup orange marmalade
2 tablespoons soy sauce
1/4 cup Jack Daniel's Tennessee Whiskey
1/4 teaspoon dry mustard
1/4 teaspoon garlic powder
2 tablespoons chopped dried cherries

Combine all the ingredients in a small saucepan or in a skillet with meat drippings. Bring to a boil over medium heat. Cook and stir until slightly thickened. Add a little water if it becomes too thick. **Makes about 1 cup.**

JACK DANIEL'S MOLASSES BUTTER

★★★★★★★★★★★★★★★★★★★★

1 cup butter, softened
1/4 cup molasses
1/4 cup sugar
2 tablespoons Jack Daniel's Tennessee Whiskey
Dash of Worcestershire sauce
Salt, to taste

Blend all ingredients together until smooth. Add a sprinkling of salt, to taste. Serve a dollop on cooked vegetables. Wrap securely and keep refrigerated.
Makes 1 1/4 cups.

MANGO PINEAPPLE JACK SALSA

★★★★★★★★★★★★★★★★★★★★★

2 ripe mangos, peeled and diced
1 cup chopped fresh pineapple or 1 cup canned
    pineapple tidbits, drained
1/4 cup chopped red or green onion
1/4 cup chopped cilantro
2 jalapeno peppers, seeded and minced
2 tablespoons Jack Daniel's Tennessee Whiskey
1 tablespoon sugar
1 tablespoon fresh lime juice
1/4 teaspoon salt

Combine all ingredients in a medium bowl. Blend well.
Chill before serving. **Makes 3 cups.**

HOLIDAY AMBROSIA

★★★★★★★★★★★★★★★★★★★★★

8 large navel oranges
3/4 cup sugar
1 1/2 cups grated coconut
Additional fresh fruits like pineapple chunks, grapes or
    kiwi slices, pomegranate seeds, optional

Peel the oranges and carefully remove the orange
sections cutting away all the white membrane. If you're
in a hurry, just slice the peeled oranges into rounds,
then in half. Toss with sugar and coconut in a large
bowl. Add additional fruit as you like. Chill before
serving. **Makes 10 servings.**

THIS SALSA SURE ISN'T A TRADITIONAL
Tennessee recipe, but it reminds me of how much
my own cooking has been influenced by cooks, ingredients, and cooking styles from around the world.
Beyond our own everyday pecans and peaches,
Jack Daniel's complements spicy and fruity flavors
in foods I'd never even heard of as a child, like this
exotic salsa. Make it whenever soft ripe mangos are
available and you're in the mood for grilled salmon
or shrimp. It's a wonderful accompaniment to the
Grilled and Glazed Salmon (see page 130) and
Jack's Sweet Hot Glazed Shrimp (see page 134).

MOTHER AND I ARE PURISTS ABOUT
many things, but not ambrosia. In addition to the
required sweet oranges and grated coconut, you
can add pineapple, grapes, or even kiwi. I'm especially fond of the sparkle of pomegranate seeds.
Of course, you can add a little Jack Daniel's.
This colorful sweet fruit dish, always served in
a gleaming cut crystal bowl, is an absolute holiday requirement. Adjust the sugar to your liking.

Things Taste Better with Jack

A brainstorm session around the kitchen table is behind this list meant to inspire you while manning the stove.

SAVORY FLAVORS

Grilled Meats—Beef, Pork, Lamb, Chicken
Deglazed Pan Drippings from Pan-Frying Beef, Pork, or Chicken
Au Jus Pan Drippings from Roasted Meats
Barbecue Sauces
Hot Wings
Sweet Potatoes
Winter Squash
Salmon with Sweet Teriyaki Sauce
Buttery Sautéed Mushrooms
Creamy Rich Foie Gras
Blue Cheese Dips and Spreads
Liver Pâté
Shrimp, Crab, and Lobster—Barbecued or in a Creamy Sauce
Sweet and Savory Meatballs or Sausages
French Onion Soup
Creamy Mushroom Bisque
Cocktail Sauce
Glazed Duckling or Goose
Venison and all Kinds of Game
Cranberry Relish
Fried Apples
Baked Beans
Sweet Relishes and Chutneys
Chili
Sugar-Glazed Baked Ham
Beef Stew
Caramelized Onions

SWEET FLAVORS

Flaming Warm Fruits like Bananas, Apples, or Peaches
Caramel Sauce
Pecan Praline
Dried Fruits
Fresh Fruits
Crème Anglaise and Boiled Custard
Buttery Baked or Sautéed Apple Desserts
Gingerbread
Chocolate Sauces, Cakes and Ice Cream
Rich Sponge Cake Trifle or Tiramisu
Desserts with all Kinds of Nuts
Pecan Pie
Bread Pudding
Poached Pears or Peaches
Maple Syrup-Flavored Desserts
Anything Flavored with Vanilla
Fruitcake--Soak the Cakes in Jack Instead of Brandy
Coffee Desserts
Fresh or Dried Figs
Sweetened Whipped Cream
Pumpkin or Sweet Potato Pie
Cheesecake

Index

★ ★ ★ ★ ★ ★ ★ ★ ★ ★ ★ ★ ★ ★

ABOUT THE AUTHORS

LYNNE TOLLEY, great-grandniece of Jack Daniel, is the proprietress of Miss Mary Bobo's Boarding House in Lynchburg, Tennessee. For more than twenty years, she has been serving midday dinner to visitors from around the world and traveling the world as ambassador for Jack Daniel's Tennessee Whiskey.

MINDY MERRELL is a food writer, columnist and cookbook author. She lives in Nashville, Tennessee.

Authors Mindy Merrell, left, and Lynne Tolley on Miss Mary's back steps